Making Words REAL

Learn how to tap into the power of imagery, communication, and collaboration to make vocabulary building fun and meaningful! Research has proven that students with a larger, more nuanced vocabulary become more proficient readers, writers, critical thinkers, and learners, making them more likely to succeed in academic environments. In this new book from Joanne M. Billingsley, an award-winning teacher and educational consultant, you will discover how to help your K–12 students expand their academic vocabulary across the content areas.

Topics include:

- ◆ using card sorts and video trailers to make vocabulary-building interactive;
- ◆ expanding your teaching strategies to support ELLs and early readers;
- ◆ building students' word knowledge through emblematic and iconic gestures;
- ◆ writing and asking scaffolded questions to get all students engaged with academic vocabulary;
- ◆ and much, much more!

The book also features sample teacher-to-student dialogues to demonstrate how to talk about words, as well as games and activities that motivate students and help word meanings stick. No matter what subject area you teach, your students will benefit from the exciting and powerful strategies in this book.

Joanne M. Billingsley is an educational consultant, author, keynote speaker, and nationally acclaimed lecturer. She is the creator of the *Vocabulary Magic*™ process for teaching academic words, www.vocabularymagic.com.

Making Words REAL

Proven Strategies for Building Academic Vocabulary Fast

Joanne M. Billingsley

Routledge
Taylor & Francis Group

NEW YORK AND LONDON

First published 2016
by Routledge
711 Third Avenue, New York, NY 10017

and by Routledge
2 Park Square, Milton Park, Abingdon, Oxon, OX14 4RN

Routledge is an imprint of the Taylor & Francis Group, an informa business

Library of Congress Cataloging-in-Publication Data
Names: Billingsley, Joanne, author.
Title: Making words REAL : proven strategies for building academic vocabulary
    fast / by Joanne Billingsley.
Description: New York, NY : Routledge, 2016. | Includes bibliographical references.
Identifiers: LCCN 2015025500| ISBN 9781138946583 (hardback) |
    ISBN 9781138946590 (pbk.) | ISBN 9781315670713 (ebook)
Subjects: LCSH: Vocabulary—Study and teaching.
Classification: LCC LB1574.5 .B47 2016 | DDC 372.44—dc23
LC record available at http://lccn.loc.gov/2015025500

ISBN: 978-1-138-94658-3 (hbk)
ISBN: 978-1-138-94659-0 (pbk)
ISBN: 978-1-315-67071-3 (ebk)

Typeset in Palatino
by Apex CoVantage, LLC

In loving memory of my parents Mary Agnes and Billy, whose unconditional love and steadfast support allowed me . . . to be me.

For eight special points of light in my life: my husband Lee, children—Anne, Michael, and Matthew, and grandchildren—Julia, Ben, Eleanor, and Renata.

In gratitude to Marguerite Hartill, who quickly transitioned from editor to dear friend during this project.

Contents

Meet the Author

Joanne Billingsley is an award-winning teacher, consultant, author, keynote speaker, and nationally acclaimed lecturer with over 20 years of classroom teaching experience. Recognized as a gifted, articulate speaker, she guides teachers in developing and implementing specific steps that build student-centered, language-rich interactive classrooms. A featured speaker at many national and regional conferences across the country, her work combines current neuroscience discoveries with best practices in teaching to develop strategies and tools that accelerate acquisition of academic vocabulary. Joanne's philosophy is "if you grow word knowledge, world knowledge will follow."

Joanne is the founder and CEO of Billingsley Education and creator of *Vocabulary Magic™: Making Words REAL*, a process for explicitly teaching difficult-to-learn academic words. Her passion is working with administrators, teachers, and students across the country, sharing strategies that have a positive and lasting impact on teacher effectiveness and student success.

Joanne received her Bachelor of Science degree in Educational Instruction and Curriculum, and her Master's degree in School and Public Health Education from Texas A&M University in College Station, Texas. She has served as an adjunct lecturer for Texas A&M University in San Antonio, and as a national presenter for the Bureau of Education and Research. Joanne is married to Lee Billingsley and resides in San Antonio, Texas. She is the proud mother of three children: Anne, Michael, and Matthew, as well as four beautiful grandchildren, Julia, Ben, Eleanor, and Renata.

For More Information . . .

To see Joanne's workshop schedule or book her for your own event, visit her website: http:/www.jmbillingsley.com http://www.jmbillingsley.com/index.php.

To purchase Joanne's *Vocabulary Magic™* products, including card sorts and vocabulary trailers, see http://www.vocabularymagic.com.

Preface

A Look at Words and Word Knowledge

The limits to your language are the limits to your world.

(Ludwig Wittgenstein)

Words have power and value. Words shape our relationships and impact the very direction of our lives. Words allow us to communicate feelings, collect or share information, and express a point of view. Words can console, condemn, or make amends. Words give access to knowledge and knowledge provides opportunity. Knowing, owning, and choosing the right words make a *significant* difference in life and in school.

Research confirms a powerful link between word knowledge and student success. Studies show that students with a robust vocabulary are much more likely to succeed in academic environments. With a stockpile of words at the ready, students are poised to become more proficient readers, writers, listeners, and speakers. Words, tucked away in the brain, can be retrieved at any moment to comprehend complex text, acquire new information, or make insights . . . all without teacher direction. A robust vocabulary opens the door for students to participate in academic discourse and to contribute to deep and meaningful conversations.

On the other hand, limited word knowledge stands in the way and restricts academic growth and opportunities. Students lacking a broad-based knowledge of words find they don't have the tools they need to engage in higher-order thinking and learning activities in the classroom. As educators, our job is to find a way to give students the tools they need to navigate the often complex texts they will encounter over time in all of their subjects.

Helping students develop strong, precise vocabulary is a vitally important task for all teachers, regardless of grade level or content area. In a very real sense, all content-area teachers are language teachers, just as all standardized state tests—in all content areas—are language assessments. Developing and implementing effective strategies to build academic language skills can shrink the *word knowledge gap* and raise *achievement levels* dramatically.

For decades we have known that word knowledge is strongly linked to school success, and recent studies continue to document persistent gaps in vocabulary. A 2012 study by the NAEP (National Assessment of Educational Progress) described the gaps in word knowledge for economically disadvantaged students in one word . . . *stark*. Stark is a frightening word when applied in this context. Word knowledge gaps appear early, often measurable in pre-kindergarten or kindergarten and persist as students move through their school years (White, Graves, & Slaters 1990). In one study, linguistically "poor" first-grade students knew approximately 5,000 words; linguistically "rich" first-graders knew about 20,000 words (Moats, 2001). As educators, we must narrow and ultimately eliminate these gaps in word knowledge. Fortunately, if we focus on identifying and implementing highly effective strategies, we can!

When teachers implement effective vocabulary strategies, students respond rapidly. It takes a teacher who is willing to commit to learning and understanding the value of these strategies in order to challenge and encourage students to believe in the power of words. To employ targeted, effective word strategies, teachers must intentionally select and explicitly teach academic vocabulary. For students who struggle and stumble to keep up with academic demands, these strategies make a significant difference. They not only help students learn new words, but they prepare students to decode complex text and complicated information at an impressive rate. When the impediments of unfamiliar words are removed, word comprehension and word usage make sense. Words can be tapped, almost subconsciously, and students no longer struggle. They *own* their words, and now they can make measureable strides in school and in life.

To prepare students with enriching word strategies, each chapter in this book introduces a highly effective strategy for boosting academic word knowledge. Specific, detailed steps are outlined so that teachers can build language-rich, interactive classrooms. Implementing these strategies will dramatically increase opportunities for students to listen, speak, read, and write using core academic vocabulary.

So let's get started . . . let's discover how to make words REAL . . . so real, in fact, that students readily understand them and routinely use them when reading, writing, listening, and speaking!

PART I
Strategies for Building Academic Vocabulary

1

Vocabulary Magic™: Billingsley's Six Steps to Building Academic Vocabulary—Using Card Sorts and Trailers

Teacher Journal

Educators and friends have frequently asked me, "What was your inspiration for *Vocabulary Magic*™? How did you discover the six-step process?" When asked those questions, I always like to think, "It wasn't what, it was who." And, I always like to share the story about a young man I met in 2009. His name was Jorge, and I worked with him for three days in an attempt to prepare him for his semester biology exam. These three days forever changed my thinking about how to teach new vocabulary to students.

Jorge was eighteen years old when we met, and he was attending a "last-chance" charter school for dropouts. Like so many of his fellow classmates, Jorge had plenty of obstacles in his way to success. He had children of his own, a criminal record, a part-time job, and a long list of learning deficiencies.

On our first day together, I was charged with helping Jorge review key biology vocabulary. Side by side we sat at the table, and I asked him what his usual strategy was for learning new words in science. He quickly reached into his backpack and proudly pulled out a large stack of index cards with a taut rubber band stretched around them. When I say large stack, I mean a really large stack! On the face of every card, he had carefully written each new biology term. On the reverse side, a glossary definition was written. In some instances, Jorge had even sketched a small picture. I was optimistic when I saw all the hard work and effort he had put into making his vocabulary flashcards. Even more encouraging was the condition of the cards. The corners of the cards were curled, and the paper was soft from repeated handling. My optimism, however, quickly faded.

As I began to quiz Jorge about the vocabulary, it became apparent that he could not read many of the definitions and knew little about the words he had so dutifully written on the index cards. His pride soon turned to embarrassment and then frustration. I remember thinking, "My gosh, these words might just as well be written in a foreign language." I knew I needed to search for a better strategy to help him learn. To encourage him, I said, "OK, Jorge, I think I just discovered something really important about you. Your brain is wired a lot like mine. It doesn't care much for words, but instead, it has a strong preference for pictures. So tomorrow we are going to try something different."

That evening I created my first Card Sort: nine words, nine pictures, and nine simple definitions. The next day, Jorge and I met and we began our lesson by saying the new words out loud. Then, we quickly picked up the picture cards. First, I asked him to use details to describe each picture. He was encouraged to think and talk about the picture, asking himself, "Does this picture remind me of anything I've learned or experienced?" Next, I asked him to make a guess about which vocabulary word might match each picture. There was no penalty for being wrong, but he had to attempt to explain his matches. After he matched all the pictures and words, he read the definition cards (not glossary definitions but student-friendly definitions), one at a time. This time, I asked him to attempt to match the definition with a picture and vocabulary term. At one point, we laughed out loud. He had three pictures under one word, and he declared, "I'm guessing two of those are wrong . . . right?"

Working until all the cards had been placed on the table, it was time to provide Jorge with some resources . . . a textbook and a laptop . . . to let him check his matches. Then he could make any corrections he thought appropriate. To conclude our lesson, I reviewed the matches with him. This gave him feedback and a final opportunity for questions and/or corrections.

I recognized the power of the strategy we were using when I administered his first assessment. I would say one of the new words from the Card Sort, and Jorge was to close his eyes and try to picture the word. Next, I listened as he described the "picture in his mind" that matched each word. The detailed descriptions he provided absolutely astonished me. But, what was even more amazing was how those images could lead him to the specific information we had discussed earlier in our lesson. Even Jorge was amazed at how much he could remember. He kept saying, "Wow, how is it that I can remember these details? I don't really feel like I have been studying these words. We just described them and talked about them." I joked with him saying, "I'm not entirely sure, but let's keep doing it because it seems to work like magic!" For Jorge, it felt like magic, and it was inspiring to see how his success created such a sense of pride for him.

That is how it started . . . sitting side-by-side with a young man named Jorge . . . both of us desperate to find a way to learn new vocabulary. After two years of arduous field-testing, and repeated "tweaking," *Vocabulary Magic™: 6 Steps to Building Academic Vocabulary* emerged as a powerful tool for teaching difficult-to-learn academic words. It is my gift to all the teachers and students who struggle to stay on grade level by mastering the mountain of new words they encounter year after year. I hope you and your students enjoy using the *Vocabulary Magic™* six-step process, and I hope you too experience a "Jorge . . . this is like magic" moment.

Vocabulary Magic™—Making Words Real!

Most teachers have watched this scenario unfold in the classroom after assigning a group project: Students are placed into cooperative learning groups to complete an activity. After the directions have been given and students are instructed to begin, two distinctly different personalities begin to emerge. The high-achieving, confident students exert control, taking over much of the responsibility for completing the task. The less confident students, those with language and/or learning deficiencies, push back and are reluctant to engage. They perceive their abilities as inadequate, and they fear ridicule or failure if they interact with high-achieving students. With the best intentions, teachers verbally encourage total participation during group work. However, total participation is seldom achieved. Repeatedly, the same students are "left on the sidelines," unable or unwilling to engage, try, or learn.

Vocabulary Magic™ Card Sort procedures ensure that all students participate equally. The step-by-step instructions are easy to implement, and the benefits students derive from the Card Sort challenge are enormous. Some of the benefits include:

1. opportunities to work in and develop small learning communities where students offer and receive support from one another;
2. a dramatic increase in student-to-student opportunities for listening, speaking, reading, and writing in small groups;

3. the availability of illustrations, teaching diagrams, and concise definitions that support student understanding and retention of new words (see Figure 1.1);
4. structured opportunities to relate to new words and to discuss prior knowledge/life experiences within a small group;
5. the availability of sentence stems to support speaking and writing in complete sentences;
6. encouragement and support in taking academic risks as well as giving and listening to different points of view;
7. the availability of immediate feedback followed by an opportunity for self-correction;
8. continued opportunities for students to play word games and to use new words in extension activities.

The power of the *Vocabulary Magic*™ six-step process becomes apparent when watching and listening to students engaged in Card Sort activities (instructions for creating effective Card Sorts follow on page 24). The easiest way to begin is to start by dropping the Card Sort bags on student desks, guide students using the instructions provided, and enjoy the richness of the conversations you are guaranteed to hear.

Figure 1.1

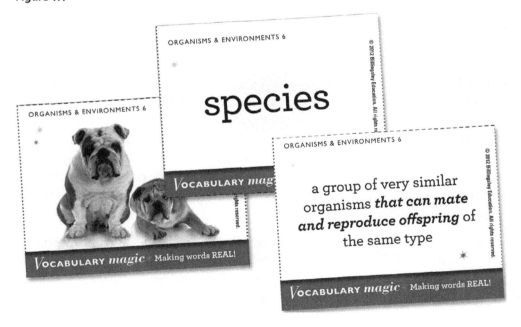

ORGANISMS & ENVIRONMENTS 6

species

ORGANISMS & ENVIRONMENTS 6

Vocabulary *magic* — Making words REAL!

ORGANISMS & ENVIRONMENTS 6

a group of very similar organisms *that can mate and reproduce offspring* of the same type

Vocabulary *magic* — Making words REAL!

Remember, no shortcuts . . . each step should be followed, or the magic disappears!

DID YOU KNOW? . . .

The National Reading Panel's review (2000) identified five basic approaches to vocabulary instruction that should be used concurrently:

- ◆ **Explicit Instruction:** This includes difficult words and words that are not part of students' everyday experiences.
- ◆ **Indirect Instruction:** This includes exposure to a wide range of reading materials.
- ◆ **Multimedia Methods:** This includes going beyond the text to incorporate a visual stimulus, e.g. using the computer or sign language.
- ◆ **Capacity Methods:** This includes focusing on making reading an automatic activity.
- ◆ **Association Methods**: This includes encouraging learners to draw connections between familiar and unfamiliar words.

Vocabulary Magic™—Six Steps for Using Card Sorts

Step 1: Sort It

Sort It provides a safe beginning for all students—the confident students as well as struggling or reluctant learners. In fact, even a beginning speaker, one new to the English language, is likely to grab the bag of new vocabulary words and get started!

How does it work? Each Card Sort consists of 27 cards: nine vocabulary words, nine companion images, and nine definitions or word descriptions. Working in groups of three, the first student picks up the Card Sort vocabulary bag, removes the cards, and carefully sorts them into three separate and neat stacks. There will be one stack of words or terms, one stack of picture cards, and a final stack of definition cards. After the cards are sorted into three stacks, the picture cards are returned to the bag; students will work with these cards next. The definition cards are pushed to the side; they will be used later in the activity.

Note: Card Sort products are available from my website: www.voca bularymagic.com or you can make them yourself by using the template in Appendix D.

Frequently Asked Questions

What is the best group size for a Card Sort?

Based on my field testing, I recommend that students work in groups of three. Generally, groups of three generate ample discussion and provide plenty of opportunity for the expression of multiple points of view. Larger groups tend to limit opportunities for involvement. The number three seems to be the optimal group size. It is also important to note that three students working together should always sit shoulder-to-shoulder, side-by-side. The reason? If students sit facing each other, some students will have to view the cards upside-down, and this is not the ideal situation.

Should I assign groups or allow students to form their own groups?

Students love to have choice in the classroom. When students are permit-ted to select their own groups, enthusiasm for an activity soars! There is a certain amount of safety and comfort for students when they are able to select group members personally. Remember, students are required to read aloud, offer opinions, and take academic risks. Fear of embarrassment or put-downs can inhibit participation, but allowing students to select their own groups increases motivation and enthusiasm for an activity. There-fore, I initially allow students to select their own groups, but I monitor groups for compatibility and progress. I make adjustments as needed.

As students become comfortable during the *Vocabulary Magic*™ pro-cess, I request students to regroup and select different partners for repeat practices. This allows students to start again within their own comfort zone. Students can move into other groups later where they will find new challenges and different points of view.

DID YOU KNOW? . . .

Direct instruction of specifically targeted words is a critical compo-nent of an effective vocabulary program and has a solid research base (Beck, Perfetti, & McKeown, 1982). Specific word instruction refers to vocabulary instruction that enables students to develop in-depth knowledge of important words—that is, for students to have "ready-to-access" information about the words and definitions in their memory banks when reading. While intentional, explicit instruction can benefit all students, and is especially important for students who have not developed the decoding and comprehension skills necessary for reading grade-level academic text.

What should I do if students begin spreading the cards and matching them without sorting the cards first?

The first step, sorting the cards and working with the picture cards, is critical. If students are allowed to quickly match cards without following the procedures, the most knowledgeable students will exert control, and they will be anxious to show what they already know. The power of *Vocabulary Magic*™ is in creating structured, student-to-student conversations using the cards. To ensure total participation and to generate academic conversations about the new terms, each step must be meticulously followed and enforced. If students skip any step in the process, they are required to pick up all cards, return them to the bag, and begin again. Be firm and consistent about these steps; make sure students honor the correct process.

What Research Has to Say

Motivation for a task increases when students feel some sense of autonomy in the learning process, and it declines when students feel they have no voice or choice. Giving your students options can be as simple as letting them pick their own partners (Reeve & Hyungshim, 2006).

Frequently Asked Questions

How many times should students repeat each Card Sort?

Short, frequent study sessions spread out over time are most efficient; this is a phenomenon known as the distributed practice effect (Baddeley & Longman, 1978). With this in mind, I recommend the following steps:

◆ First day: Students get initial exposure to new vocabulary words using the Card Sort. Step-by-step instructions must be followed.

◆ Second day: Students review the words by repeating the Card Sort. Then, they select and complete either the Word Journal in Appendix B or write sentences incorporating the new words using the Sentence Stems for Students found in Appendix C.

◆ Two days later: Students repeat the Card Sort for the third time. This is called a Quick Sort because matches are made quickly with less discussion. Basically, this is a time for a knowledge check. Students play one or more of the recommended Games and Extension Activities in Chapter 7 using the cards provided.

◆ One week later: Students are given an additional opportunity to play one or more of the recommended Games and Extension Activities.

◆ Approximately two weeks after initial exposure, students complete one additional review as a practice opportunity.

Research confirms that a practice schedule with the above parameters maximizes retention (Bahrick, Bahrick, Bahrick, & Bahrick, 1993). Don't buy into the "I already know all these words" refrain. Require students to do the Card Sort and provide challenging extension activities for them when they finish. Research confirms the importance of practicing beyond mastery in order for skills to be hardwired or permanent.

Approximately how many new words should I attempt to pre-teach during an average school year?

What Research Has to Say

The number of new words that students need to learn each year is exceedingly large. On average, students need to learn 2,000 to 3,000 new words each year from third grade onward, about 6–8 words per day (Anderson & Nagy, 1992). Although it is impossible to teach all the new words students need to learn, it is useful to provide direct instruction for some words. Research estimates that students can be explicitly taught some 400 words per school year (Beck, McKeown, & Kucan, 2002).

Vocabulary Magic™ Card Sorts are highly engaging, and the process for using them is based on neuroscience research studies that have revealed how the brain learns and remembers. As a result, this method can *stretch* student capacity for learning, understanding, and retaining new words. In many content areas, the predominant method of vocabulary instruction utilizes the unit vocabulary word list. Students look up and copy definitions, make flash cards, create graphic organizers, do crossword puzzles, write context clue sentences, etc. The problem is that these strategies are frequently inadequate and inefficient. Students can create stacks of vocabulary flash cards and countless graphic organizers, never actually using the new words they are attempting to learn when speaking or writing.

Rote memorization of words and definitions is the least effective instructional method for building vocabulary, resulting in poor long-term retention. Students and teachers experience frustration when students memorize words for a test and forget half of them by the following week. For new words to become real—part of a student's productive vocabulary—they must use them in conversation and in writing.

Vocabulary Magic™ Card Sorts offer a friendly, fun environment with dramatic increases in opportunities to use new words when listening, speaking, reading, and writing. Card Sorts offer a more effective, efficient method for explicit pre-teaching of selected vocabulary . . . and students love using them!

Teacher–Student Dialogue

Enrique: Why do I have to follow these instructions? We just want to match the words, pictures, and definitions quickly. We already know some of them. We can finish the Card Sort much faster our own way.

Teacher: Using special neuroscience or "brain tricks," the *Vocabulary Magic*™ Card Sorts will help you learn and remember new vocabulary words quickly with what feels like little effort. But this only occurs if all steps in the process are followed and if you are committed to practicing the words several times. Remember, you will have hundreds of new words to learn during each school year. Following the directions will help imprint or stamp these new words into your memory bank so you can recall them and use them for many years to come. It's like magic! No more learning words just for the quiz and then forgetting them. With *Vocabulary Magic*™ Card Sorts, new words become REAL WORDS, and they become part of your working vocabulary.

DID YOU KNOW? . . .

Vocabulary is a strong indicator of reading success (Biemiller, 2003). Established research from the 1970s shows the decline of reading comprehension in children—aged eight and above—resulting from a lack of vocabulary knowledge (Becker, 1977). Primarily, it was caused by a lack of learning opportunities, not a lack of natural ability. Chall, Jacobs, and Baldwin (1990) also found that disadvantaged students showed a decline in reading comprehension because their limited vocabulary restricted textual understanding.

Tips to Consider for English Language Learners (ELLs)

✓ Allow ELLs to use native language dictionaries and resources if needed.
✓ Allow ELLs to select their own groups; it ensures a comfort level that reduces anxiety.
✓ Have ELLs interact with L1 and L2 dominant peers during Card Sort activities.
✓ Place the *Vocabulary Magic*™ bag into the hands of an ELL student at the start of the Card Sort to encourage participation.
✓ Consider reducing the number of new words introduced at one time. For example, a set of nine words might be divided into sets of four and five words for the initial sort. As students master these words, they can tackle all nine words together.

Step 2: Say It

With the picture cards tucked away in the bag and the definition cards pushed aside, students focus their attention on the new words in this Card Sort. Students put the new terms side by side, horizontally across the table (see Figure 1.2).

Figure 1.2

| motion | frame of reference | constant speed | speed | friction | inertia | net force | balanced force | unbalanced force |

After the cards are laid out, the teacher will say each word; the students will repeat the word, locate the word in the lineup, and point to the word with their fingers. Difficult-to-pronounce words should be repeated more than once, and students should have multiple opportunities to hear and repeat the words.

In addition, as each word is identified, teachers should share a snippet of information or novel fact about the new word. Adding gestures as the information is shared will help hold student attention and increase comprehension. Do not miss this opportunity to have fun with the new word. For example, when introducing the terms *balanced force* and *unbalanced force*, the teacher might stretch his/her arms out to the side, tipping back and forth in a seesaw motion. When modeling *balanced forces,* the teacher will eventually steady the seesaw and become balanced. While modeling *unbalanced forces* the teacher continues to tip back and forth until pretending to tip over. Students enjoy the gesturing and gesturing makes words far more comprehensible for students, particularly ELLs. And as you will have discovered in Chapter 4, gesturing encodes information in the brain in a unique manner, increasing both recall and accuracy.

It is also valuable during this step to tell students what a word *does not* represent. This is particularly helpful for words with multiple meanings. Students hearing the term *net force*, for example, might be picturing a device used for capturing insects being fiercely swung through the air. The teacher can clarify by gesturing and saying, "In the term *net force*, the word *net* is not referring to a device for catching insects. Here the word *net* means total, added, or combined."

Reluctance to participate in the Card Sort diminishes as students grow comfortable hearing the proper pronunciation of unfamiliar words. Fear of not knowing how to pronounce a new word is frequently the most significant deterrent to learning and using the word in conversation. During the course of completing the Card Sort, students will hear, read, and say the new words multiple times. With each correct pronunciation, their confidence increases.

Frequently Asked Questions

Is it necessary to provide a pronunciation guide for the new words?
Because textbook glossaries and dictionaries provide students with pronunciation guides, I do not include them in the Card Sort. Remember, students will hear and say the words before they start the Card

Sort. I recommend that teachers monitor students during the Card Sort activity to ensure proper pronunciation of new words. It sounds like this:

The teacher says: I hear several students struggling with the correct pronunciation of the word *photosynthesis*. Let's break this new word into syllables and practice saying it together.

The teacher says: I see the prefix/root/suffix . . . remember it means . . .

You've encouraged teachers to share information about words during the "say it" step, but how much information should I share?

Share a single fun fact or simple gesture, or clarify a word with a multiple meaning, but *do not define the word*. Sharing too much information diminishes the challenge for the Card Sort. Don't spoil the challenge with too much information!

Tips to Consider for ELLs

✓ Monitor ELL word pronunciation and provide support.
✓ Support ELLs in making connections to relevant cognates. Teachers might ask, "Do you know any words in your native language similar to . . ."
✓ Discuss word parts such as prefix, root, or suffix when appropriate.

Step 3: Describe It

Reaching into the bag, a student removes one picture card. The student then shows the picture to the group and proceeds to describe the image, providing as many details as possible.

The student says, "In this picture I see . . ." *After fully describing the picture*, the student uses the following sentence stem in an attempt to match the picture with one of the vocabulary words on the table. The student says, **"I think this picture might match the word . . . because . . ."**

Note: The sentence stem includes the word *because* to encourage students to explain their matches. As they explain, students probe prior knowledge, think about relationships, and examine previous experiences. With one-third to one-half of the human brain devoted to visual processing (Medina, 2008), you can be sure that when students closely examine images and explain matches, minds are working.

After the first student matches the picture card with a word card on the table, the bag is passed to the next student. The process is repeated until all pictures have been described and matched to one of the vocabulary words. Remember, only one picture card is removed at a time. Each picture must be *described in detail* to the other group members and an attempted match must be made and explained. More detail usually translates to deeper understanding and better retention. Reinforce this . . . during a student's turn (when they are describing a card), other group members are *not permitted to talk.* Remind students, "The one who describes must decide." Partners are not permitted to offer any input at this point!

After all nine picture cards have been described and placed, the group can have an open discussion about matches, share ideas, experiences, and offer suggestions. The group is free to make any agreed upon corrections by moving the picture cards. Provide ample time for debate, sharing, and self-correction. Student dialogue at this point will be focused on academic words and content. You do not want to interrupt the conversations. Students must verbalize to internalize! We want students listening, speaking, thinking, and self-correcting. Just observe, listen, and enjoy!

Student-to-Student Dialogue

A student removes the following picture card (see Figure 1.3):

Roger: On this card I see two different pictures. The first one is a picture of a man pushing on a wall. It looks like he is pushing really hard, with a lot of effort. Under this picture it says *non-example.* The second picture shows two people lifting a box. With bent knees, they pick up the box from the floor and stand, lifting the box waist high. Under the box is an arrow that points upward. The arrow might indicate the direction the box moves, or it could represent that the pair is applying an upward force on the box. Next to this picture it says example. "I think that this picture might match the word . . . because . . ."

Note: Detail is important. Not only does it encourage students to look closely at what they see, it deepens understanding, improves retention, and provides important opportunities to use language. Encourage details, details, details, and even more details!

Figure 1.3

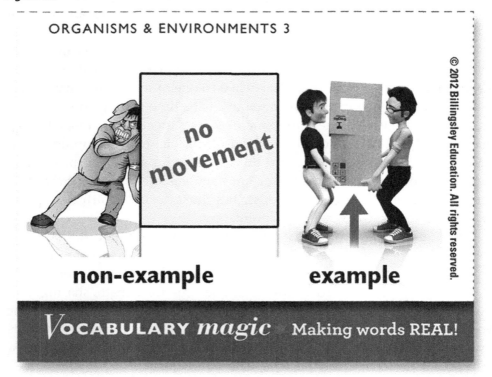

ORGANISMS & ENVIRONMENTS 3

no movement

non-example   example

*V*OCABULARY *magic*   Making words REAL!

Frequently Asked Questions

What can the teacher do to encourage students to use sentence stems?

In the beginning, students sometimes forget to use the stems. Using the stems ensures that students speak in complete sentences using academic vocabulary. Provide each group with a copy of the sentence stems printed on a half-sheet of paper. If groups are not using the stems, simply tap on the copy to remind them. With a little prompting and practice, using the stems will become routine.

If a student places a picture card under the incorrect vocabulary word, should group members attempt to correct the error or give input?

It is important for the student describing the picture to make the match without input from the group. Remember, students must say, "I think this picture might match . . ." The sentence stem gives students permission to take an academic risk, and to use prior knowledge and experience to verbalize the description. If other students in the group are allowed to intervene, the more capable students will make most of the decisions, diminishing participation and learning.

It is possible for two pictures to end up under a single vocabulary word. If that happens, the group can discuss the possibility of moving one of the pictures, but only after all picture cards have been placed. If they cannot come to an agreement about moving a card, it is perfectly all right to leave the card where it was originally placed.

DID YOU KNOW? . . .

In a landmark 2003 study, researchers Betty Hart and Todd Risley identified "remarkable differences" in the early vocabulary experiences of young children. Hart described the results of their observations by stating: "Simply in words heard, the average child on welfare was having half as much experience per hour (616 words per hour) as the average working-class child (1,251 words per hour) and less than one-third that of the average child in a professional family (2,153 words per hour)." It was estimated that children from high-income families were exposed to 30 million more words than children from families on welfare. Subsequent studies have shown that these differences in language and interaction experiences have a lasting effect on a child's performance in school.

If a student has limited background knowledge, should they be encouraged to guess when placing a picture?
Absolutely! Remind students fearful of making mistakes that this is a pre-teaching strategy. The expectation is that word knowledge may be limited when working with challenging academic vocabulary. The objective is to grow word knowledge. The process will reveal what you don't know . . . so that you can learn it!

What Research Has to Say
It is generally accepted that pictures are more memorable than words, and most people are familiar with and agree with the expression, "A picture is worth a thousand words." In fact, a single picture can contain enough information to replace several sentences. In addition, pictures are more universally understood, and they are not restricted to the knowledge of

any specific language. Memory theorists confirm that pictures are better remembered than words on recognition tests (Brady, Konkle, Alvarez, & Oliva, 2008).

Paivio's Dual Code Theory (Paivio & Csapo, 1973) states that when pictures are studied, they elicit visual mental imagery and a verbal label, and therefore two representations or codes are stored in the memory. Words, however, do not automatically elicit a picture or mental image, and thus they result in a relatively impoverished memory representation. Pictures are so effective at imprinting memory that theorists have given this phenomenon a name, Picture Superiority Effect, or PSE.

Tips to Consider for ELLs

✓ Allow students to describe the pictures in their native language if they are beginning or intermediate speakers, but encourage them to use English words when possible.
✓ Have students use the Sentence Stems for Students in Appendix C to support speaking in complete sentences.

Step 4: Read It

After all pictures are matched, students place the definition cards into the plastic bag, as was done in Step 2. The process continues, with each definition card being removed one at a time. The student removing the card *must read the definition aloud* to the group members and use the following stem to explain the match:

The student says: I think this definition might match the word . . . and this picture . . . because . . .

Again, students are asked to explain their matches. Frequently they will find "clues" to facilitate their success in both the pictures and the definitions. The dialogue may sound like this:

Student-to-Student Dialogue

Samantha: I think this definition might match the term DNA and this picture because it describes something long and twisted, and the picture looks like a twisted ladder (see Figure 1.4). I think they call it a double helix in our science book.

Edward: I see what you mean. If you untwisted it, it would look like a ladder.

Figure 1.4

Frequently Asked Questions

How can I accommodate for struggling readers who might be reluctant to read aloud?
Remember, if students have been allowed to select their groups, they should experience a "comfort level" with group members when asked to read aloud. However, teachers can encourage more competent readers to assist and support students who read below grade level. In addition, I recommend the definitions be "student friendly," and familiar words should be used when possible. This increases both participation and understanding.

What if some students are distracted or not listening while the definition card is being read aloud?
First, require the students doing the reading to lay the definition card on the table, where it is clearly visible to the group. Second, have the reader move his/her finger along the definition as they read. The act of pointing and tracing while reading focuses visual and auditory brain regions. The same is true when students point to pictures as they describe what they see. *It is important for the card being described or read to be seen by all group*

members. The best way to accomplish this is to have students lay them on the table (not hold them in their hand) during the process.

Tips for ELLs

✓ Allow ELLs to discuss words and matches using native and social language when working with partners.
✓ Monitor ELLs to be sure they are using the Sentence Stems for Students. For example, they should say, "In this picture I see . . ." and "I think this picture might match the word . . . because . . ."
✓ Encourage ELLs to connect new words to their own experiences inside and outside of school.

DID YOU KNOW? . . .

Research conducted by Duke and Moses (2003) concludes that reading to children and getting children to read on their own forms a foundation for vocabulary growth. Additional research shows that vocabulary growth is further supported when children read and speak at home using rich oral language.

Step 5: Check It

After students complete all matches, they can watch the Vocabulary Trailer. A Vocabulary Trailer is a teacher-generated, three-minute movie presentation that allows students to see the correct word/picture/definition matches. The information and images are incorporated into PowerPoint slides and put to music, increasing the entertainment factor. The trailer reveals the correct matches and provides *immediate feedback* for students. When the trailer is finished, students are asked to rearrange cards if they need to make corrections. Students can watch the trailer a second time, if need be. The trailer is a powerful tool, providing engaging, timely feedback to students regarding their attempted matches. But it is much, much more. Vocabulary Trailers quickly place new words in context, and they provide additional "mind-enticing" bits of information that imprint memory. Students love them and remember them!

What Research Has to Say

W. Fred Miser said, "Feedback is an objective description of a student's performance intended to guide future performance." He continued by explaining that unlike evaluation, which judges performance, feedback is the process that helps students: assesses their performance, identifies areas where they are right, and listens to tips telling them how to improve in the future.

Academic feedback is more strongly and consistently related to achievement than any other teaching behavior. This relationship is consistent regardless of grade, socioeconomic status, race, or school setting. When feedback and corrective procedures are used, most students can attain the same level of achievement as the top 20% of students.

(Bellon, Bellon, & Blank, 1992)

Frequently Asked Questions

Can a Card Sort be effective without the Vocabulary Trailer?

Teachers frequently express frustration with students' unwillingness to correct their mistakes. Using the Vocabulary Trailers greatly increases the likelihood that students will not only correct mistakes but remember the corrections. Whether it is a missed test question or a simple mistake on a worksheet, most student errors are left uncorrected. When feedback about mistakes is delayed, e.g. students waiting for a returned assignment, the feedback is of limited value. In order for feedback to be useful, it must be provided quickly. The Vocabulary Trailer allows students to receive immediate feedback after completing the Card Sort, and any mistake is promptly corrected.

Trailers can be used effectively for review and remediation without teacher assistance; they can augment interactive lectures; and they are powerful tools for learning and remembering. In addition, the trailers are highly engaging. Students see images, matching words, and definitions put to music. The trailers imprint memory in a powerful way, and they make learning new words enjoyable.

Tips for ELLs

- ✓ Allow ELLs multiple opportunities to view the Vocabulary Trailers.
- ✓ Provide ELLs with a pdf file of the trailer so they can "click" through the presentation slide by slide and discuss the contents and images.

DID YOU KNOW? . . .

Evidence from Apthorp (2006) supports and extends that cited by the National Reading Panel. Apthorp's conclusions named a solid base of evidence to support three key elements of vocabulary instruction, effective for vocabulary development and improved reading comprehension. These elements are:

- ◆ **defining and explaining** word meanings;
- ◆ **arranging frequent encounters** with new words—at least six exposures to each new word;
- ◆ **encouraging deep and active processing** of words and meanings in a range of contexts.

These strategies are effective for vocabulary development and improved reading comprehension.

Step 6: Expand It

The Vocabulary Trailer that follows each Card Sort provides much more than an opportunity to check answers and make corrections. Information in the trailer links the new word, the images, and the definitions with one other relevant piece of information in a "Did You Know? . . ." slide (see Figure 1.5). This section of the Vocabulary Trailer immediately expands the student's working knowledge of new words using images, student-friendly definitions, and new facts. This helps students make connections to the word and inspires them to think about the word in broader contexts. Now the vocabulary words form a network of meaningful and memorable knowledge.

After viewing the trailer and self-correcting, students will select or be assigned one or more extension activities to complete. The two I highly recommend are:

1. **Word Journals**: Students select words to enter in their Word Journals. The journal entry includes a picture, definition, information from the "Did You Know? . . ." section of the Vocabulary Trailers, and any other significant information students can document about a word. A template for students to use is included in Appendix B.

2. **Speaking and Writing with Stem Support**: Stem Support is used when students complete the Card Sort and view the Vocabulary Trailer. Students select from the ten sentence stems provided in Appendix C. Responses are first given verbally and then in writing. When students respond using the sentence stems, they are encouraged to:

    ◆ explore relationships between words;
    ◆ probe prior knowledge;
    ◆ state definitions in their own words;
    ◆ describe a visual representation of new words;
    ◆ connect new words with examples from their own experiences;
    ◆ speak and write with new words in complete sentences.

Tips for ELLs

✓ Recommend that ELLs create a Word Journal for each new Card Sort. These journals can provide support when reading more complex academic text. A Word Journal is also a great place for ELLs to make personal notes and record connections they make between new words and their native language.

✓ Encourage the use of sentence stems for ELLs. They provide support when speaking and reading.

Engaging in *Vocabulary Magic*™ provides a safe beginning for students who are learning new vocabulary. Students learn to categorize by sorting vocabulary cards into pictures, words, and definitions. Then, they systematically move forward and progress while learning to listen, speak, read, and write using subject-specific academic vocabulary terms.

Creating Effective Card Sorts and Trailers

Frequently Asked Questions

How many words should be included in a single Card Sort?

One of the most highly cited papers in psychology is "The magical number seven, plus or minus two: Some limits on our capacity for processing information." This paper was published in 1956 by the cognitive psychologist George A. Miller of Princeton University's Department of Psychology in *Psychological Review*. It argues that the number of objects an average human can hold in working memory, sometimes referred to as short-term memory, is 7 + 2. This is frequently called *Miller's Law*.

More recent research suggests that the number of chunks a human can recall immediately after presentation depends on the category of chunks used. For example: for digits, the magic number is about seven; for letters, the number is about six; and for words, it is about five.

Because Card Sorts are designed to challenge and improve working memory, I recommend that Card Sorts consist of nine words. When words are paired with eye-catching images and student-friendly definitions, students can have structured conversations about new vocabulary words. While doing so, working memory is exercised and strengthened.

Field testing has shown that most students in grades 3–12 can successfully handle up to nine words in a single Card Sort. Carefully selected images and concisely worded definitions on the cards greatly increase the likelihood of success. This success provides the "encouragement" needed to boost student effort and to maintain sustained participation in the activity.

How do you determine which words to include in a Card Sort?

By design, Card Sorts include two types of words: core vocabulary (brick words) and processing words (mortar words). Brick words are content-specific terms, words that are generally boldfaced and found in the glossary of the textbook. In science, for example, brick words might include *DNA*, *chromosome*, *gene*, and *mutation*. In contrast, mortar words are general-utility words that hold the content-specific technical words together. Examples of mortar words within a science unit on genetics might include words such as *dominant, characteristic, trait,* and *diversity.*

In designing a Card Sort, you might consider using seven core vocabulary words and two processing words per Card Sort. In doing so, this arrangement provides students with a chunk of information about the right size to chew on. If students bite off more than they can chew, things get stuck before they can be processed! Teachers and students can decide to separate Card Sorts into smaller chunks, e.g. with groups of four to five words, when necessary. ELLs and special needs students may benefit from working with fewer words.

Remember, it is not realistic to provide direct instruction for all new content-area words that students need to learn each year. Careful selection is recommended using the following guidelines adapted from Cooper (1997).

- The selected words will be frequently encountered in text and content areas.
- The selected words are important to understanding the core content or main idea.
- The selected words are *not* a part of the students' prior knowledge.
- The selected words are unlikely to be learned independently through the use of context and/or structural analysis.

DID YOU KNOW? . . .

Based on research, Fisher and Blachnowicz (2005) recommend that teachers:

- **ensure** a **word-rich** learning environment;
- **address** vocabulary learning as a **distinct area** in the curriculum;
- **select** appropriate words for planned teaching and reinforcement, e.g. words that have similar parts, such as medicine/medical/medicate.

How do I select images, and where do I get them?

Selecting the right image can prove to be a challenging task. While there may not be a perfect image for each new word, some images are more powerful at imprinting memory and conveying meaning than others. An aspect I always consider is novelty. The brain loves novelty. Novelty captures attention and generates questions. Remember, students will be asked to describe the images in detail to their partners; therefore I like to use images that include interesting detail. Some images provide detail that facilitates the match. For example, if the definition of a *chromosome* is an *X-shaped structure made up of DNA*, I want to make sure the picture is distinguishable as an X-shaped structure. When definitions and images provide built-in clues, students read and examine them more carefully. Since the object is to get students to learn and carefully examine pictures for clues that lead to a correct match, the built-in clues should offer support and an opportunity to analyze. Sometimes the clues can be there; sometimes they may not be. The brain loves a surprise!

Should I use the glossary definitions in the text on the cards?

Don't get me wrong, I love having a glossary in the back of a textbook for student reference, but sometimes these technically accurate definitions are not student-friendly. The definitions in a Card Sort need to be concise, and they need to utilize student-friendly language. Don't attempt to include a comprehensive definition for every card; instead, get to the main idea quickly. Students will add to this basic definition as they encounter the new vocabulary words in more complex text. Just feel comfortable knowing that the Card Sort definition provides a mental cognitive hook to which expanded information can be attached.

What do I need to create an effective vocabulary trailer?

Creating a highly effective Vocabulary Trailer might be easier than you think. If you have created an effective Card Sort, the work is almost complete. Half of the slides in the PowerPoint trailer will utilize the words, pictures, and definitions from the Card Sort.

The creative and fun challenge is in generating the "Did You Know? . . ." slides. On these slides, you will provide students with a surprise. Basically, the surprise is to give students a fact, or information, that is novel or unique about the word they are learning. For example,

Figure 1.5

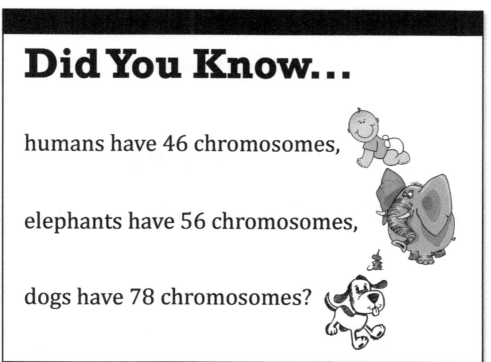

Did You Know...

humans have 46 chromosomes,

elephants have 56 chromosomes,

dogs have 78 chromosomes?

after learning about the word *chromosome,* the "Did You Know? . . ." slide might offer this piece of surprising information: All organisms do not have the same number of chromosomes; humans have 46, elephants 56, and dogs 78! (See Figure 1.5.)

Note: To see a sample Card Sort and companion Vocabulary Trailer go to: www.vocabularymagic.com.

2

Modified *Vocabulary Magic*™: Six Steps for Pre-Readers and ELLs

As outlined in Chapter 1, teachers have successfully used my six-step *Vocabulary Magic*™ process with grade-level students, but they often want to know:

◆ Which modifications work for pre-readers and beginning ELLs who struggle with reading and understanding definitions during a traditional Card Sort activity?

◆ Is there a modified version of the *Vocabulary Magic*™: *6 Steps* that I can use with all students, one that does not require the 27 cards used in a formal Card Sort activity?

These questions can be answered simply and reassuringly. With some modifications and teacher facilitation, *Vocabulary Magic*™: *6 Steps* can provide unique opportunities for pre-readers and beginning ELL students to learn the academic vocabulary they will need to succeed. As students gain skills and confidence, they can transition to the traditional six-step method. In addition, teachers can use the *modified steps* with all students to teach academic words not included in formal Card Sorts. The list of required vocabulary terms students must master is long. Reserve the traditional *Vocabulary Magic*™: *6 Steps* for the first top 100–180 *need-to-know words* and tackle the rest of the word list using a variety of other strategies. The *modified Vocabulary Magic*™: *6 Steps* described as follows, will serve as another powerful tool for building academic vocabulary and literacy skills.

This process involves two parts. Part One is called *When I See*, and Part Two is called *When I Hear*.

Part One: When I See

During Part One, students use word cards and teacher-selected images. The images are projected or posted in the classroom and students are asked to describe the images they see. The teacher-selected images replace the picture cards in a traditional word sort.

Let's examine how to prepare for Part One: When I See.

Teacher Preparation for Part One

1. Select nine key academic vocabulary terms related to a common concept. Print the nine terms on a single page (see Figure 2.1), cut out each term, and place them all in a small plastic bag that we call a Vocabulary Bag.

Figure 2.1

motion	energy	force
pull	push	magnetism
gravity	buoyant	friction

Note: Unlike a traditional Card Sort, where students work with picture, word, and definition cards, students will use only word cards for this modified version. Students work in small collaborative learning communities, as the teacher facilitates the activity by reading and guiding groups in class discussion.

2. Next, create a PowerPoint presentation that includes ten slides.

   ◆ The first slide in the PowerPoint presentation should contain a 3 x 3 table with the nine selected vocabulary terms (see Figure 2.1). For example, the nine words for this lesson are: *motion, energy, force, pull, push, magnetism, gravity, buoyant, friction*.
   ◆ Next, make nine additional slides, one for each vocabulary term and its corresponding image. Be sure to insert the two sentence stems above the image: *In this picture I see . . .* and *I think this picture might match the word . . . because . . .* (see Figure 2.2).

Now, let's examine the steps to implement Part One with students using the PowerPoint slides and teacher support.

Figure 2.2

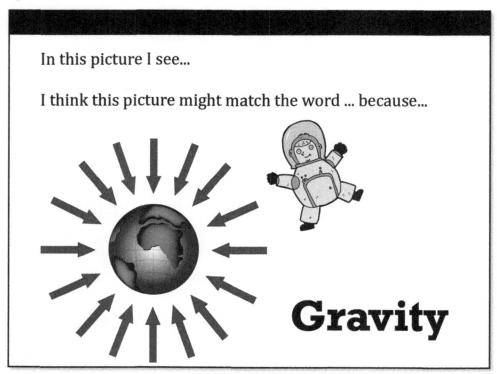

Steps for Implementing Part One
Step 1: Arrange It

Viewing the first slide, students remove the nine word cards from the Vocabulary Bag and arrange the cards on their desks to match the image projected. After the cards have been assembled, in columns and rows, each group is given a clothespin (the wooden type with a metal spring). The clothespin is passed from student to student during the lesson as they take turns. A clothespin is not essential, but it helps keep younger students on track. While passing the clothespin, they always know whose turn it is to speak and decide.

Step 2: Say It and Point to It

The teacher points to and pronounces the term on the first slide. Next, students are asked to repeat and point to the corresponding word card on their desks. Difficult-to-pronounce terms can be repeated as many times as needed. As each word is introduced, the teacher can offer small, relevant bits of information related to the new term. Incorporating gestures that correspond to the word, when possible, helps increase student understanding of the term. For example, ask students to rub their hands together vigorously, and say, "Did you know that *friction* can produce heat?" Gestures and fun snippets of information for each new term keeps students engaged, increases comprehension, and greatly enhances the lesson.

Step 3: Describe It

The teacher advances the PowerPoint to the second slide. The second slide in the presentation reveals the first image. Within each group, the student holding the clothespin will use the sentence stem and say to a partner, "In this picture I see . . ." The students then describe the projected image to their partners. During this step:

◆ Encourage students to observe and share as many details about the picture as possible with the group. Set the stage by asking students to talk about the shapes, colors, and details. For instance, they might describe what is happening in the picture, or they might tell a partner that the picture recalls something they have seen or experienced before.

◆ Tell students to use their best, most precise words to describe the image. Say, "I want you to close your eyes and see the image in your mind. Then, share those details with your partner." (See a sample student-to-student dialogue that follows.)

◆ Model for the students. Let them hear you describe a picture using the stem. As they engage in the practice, monitor student conversations to make sure they are describing and talking about the picture.

Sample Student-to-Student Dialogue

Student to partner: In this picture, I see the Earth. It looks like a ball with lots of red arrows pointing towards it. On Earth, the water is blue, and the land looks green. I also see a person in a space suit floating in space. It looks like they might be floating away from Earth. I think this picture might match the term gravity because I think gravity is what keeps us attached to the Earth so we don't float away into space. I've seen movies where astronauts are floating all around inside space ships. I don't think there is any gravity in space. (See Figure 2.2.)

Step 4: Check It

After describing the image and explaining the match, the students should clasp the selected word card with the clothespin. When all students in each group have made their selections, the teacher says, *"One, two, three, please show me."* Students hold up the term they have selected, and the teacher reads the selected words out loud or visually scans the selections to make assessments. Next, the teacher says, *"Here is the term I had in mind when I selected this image."* The teacher reveals the word as it appears (fades in) on the screen next to the image. After the answer is revealed, the teacher provides a brief explanation of the word for students. During this explanation, the teacher describes the thinking behind the definition and elaborates on the term. This provides an opportunity for students to make new links and connections to the word. (See a sample teacher–student dialogue below.)

Sample Teacher–Student Dialogue

Teacher: The red arrows represent the force of gravity, pulling objects, including us, towards the Earth. Without gravity, the ocean's waters would float off into space! You were correct if you described the astronaut as floating away from Earth. As objects get farther and farther from Earth's surface, the pull of the Earth's gravity gets weaker.

Teacher: Samantha, I noticed you and your group selected the term buoyant force for this image. Can you tell me what you were thinking
when you chose that term?

Student: We picked the words buoyant force because we think buoyant
means to float and the astronaut looked like he was floating in
space.

Teacher: Excellent observation and good thinking! You are correct; buoy-
ancy is related to floating. I selected a different image to represent buoyant force. It will be coming up soon, let's see if you can
identify it.

To keep students actively engaged, teachers can occasionally select students at random to share their descriptions with the whole class. While students share, they are encouraged to do two things: describe the image and
provide the clues they used to make a match. This provides important feedback and assessment of student thinking and learning. The more students talk
about and describe the images, the more valuable the experience. In short,
more engagement creates a more *language-rich exercise in a more language-
rich environment.*

Remember, the student who described the image must be the one to
select the term. The teacher can remind students by repeating, "The one who
describes MUST decide." Students are required to take an academic risk and
explain their thinking . . . knowing there is no penalty for being wrong. *The
partners in the group wait until the student makes a selection, and the clothespin
is placed on the word card.* If it is your turn, you must decide. Your partners
must remain silent. They may offer suggestions about the student's choice,
after a card is selected, but ultimately, the student with the clothespin gets
to decide which term is chosen. If a student mistakenly selects the wrong
term, or wants to change a decision after receiving input, it is not a problem.
Students are allowed to self-correct. *Students should learn quickly that this system does not punish mistakes but rather provides opportunities for self-correction,
growth, and exploration of words.*

After each term is discussed thoroughly, groups can place that word card
back into the Vocabulary Bag, leaving eight word cards on the desk. The
clothespin is passed to the next student, and steps 1, 2, and 3 are repeated.

Part Two: When I Hear

In Part Two of the lesson, the teacher builds on the image descriptions
by introducing synonyms, adjectives, and simple descriptive statements

connected to the images projected/posted in the classroom. This modification replaces the definition cards in a word sort.

Let's examine the steps to implement Part Two: When I Hear.

Teacher Preparation for Part Two

Create a second PowerPoint using synonyms, adjectives, or short descriptive statements for each vocabulary term. These slides should be language-rich. It is the perfect opportunity to introduce students to related words. Do not be afraid to include some challenging or unfamiliar words. Students get excited when they learn and experiment with "fancy" words they can later use to impress other students, teachers, or parents. First-graders love words like shift, flinch, recoil, relocate, shuffle, and transfer as substitutes for the word motion. When possible, select words that are fun to model (see Figures 2.3 and 2.4)!

Figure 2.3   **Figure 2.4**

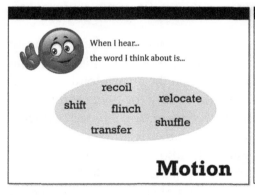 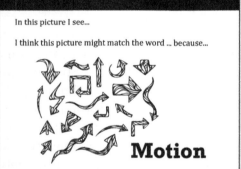

Next, let's examine the steps to implement Part Two with students using the PowerPoint slides and teacher support.

Steps for Implementing Part Two
Step 1: Read It

As each slide is presented, the teacher points to and reads the vocabulary-rich text to the entire class. If it is possible to make gestures that correspond with each word, it will increase comprehension and engage students. Sometimes the text refers back to the image used in Part One, providing clues and triggering memory. For example, for the term *gravity*, the description reads; *attached to the Earth, astronaut in space*, referring to the image shown in

Part One. The more synonyms, adjectives, and examples provided, the more connections students will be able to make.

Step 2: Pick It

After hearing the teacher read the text, the student holding the clothespin will say, "When I hear those words, I think about . . ." Then, the student will select a word from the table. Again, partners can provide feedback only after the student has made a selection.

Step 3: *Check It* and *Expand It*

The teacher calls for students to hold up the word cards they have selected. The answer is revealed, and the discussion, elaboration, and joy of discovery begins once more!

Frequently Asked Questions

What is the best way to select vocabulary for pre-readers and beginning ELL students?

Mostly, the words for pre-readers and beginning ELL students are Tier 3 words, which are best described as glossary terms or core academic vocabulary. However, they can be key processing words, sometimes called *mortar* words or *high-frequency* words that appear in academic text.

Is it too much of a stretch to expect pre-readers and beginning ELL students to learn sophisticated academic vocabulary?

Not at all! The modifications used in this section place academic words in context using images, gestures, and conversation in a well-rounded, comprehensive manner. Using these techniques simultaneously offers students a way to become familiar with challenging, difficult-to-learn vocabulary in a way that makes sense.

Would it be appropriate for teachers to use this strategy in all content areas with all students?

To practice this strategy across content-areas means that teachers work jointly. When they do, students can expect to learn academic language in any class they enter. The more they are acquainted with the process, the more comfortable they will become with it . . . and the more they will learn. Remember, the goal is to build a language-rich classroom with high levels of student participation in all classes.

3

More Strategies for Building Academic Vocabulary

Learning from our mistakes . . .

I was discussing the human skeletal system with my seventh-grade science students one morning, and I knew I had to pause to tell them about an astonishing event I witnessed that morning on the way to school. I told my students the story was about a young man on a skateboard who was hit by a car. Suddenly, I had their undivided attention.

"The story begins like this," I said. "The driver of the car, distracted while texting, jumped the curb and hit a teenage boy, damaging his spinal cord." My life-sized, human skeletal model affectionately named Flaco (which means skinny in Spanish) was positioned behind me. While re-enacting the crash scene with much animation, I lurched backward and collided with Flaco, the skeleton.

The end result was absolutely catastrophic for Flaco. He flew backward, hit my desk, and crashed to the floor . . . much like the teenage boy who was hit by the car. The metal rod running through Flaco's vertebrae snapped in two pieces and bones scattered all over the floor. His head bounced out the classroom door and into the hallway. Story interrupted! I stopped, and a student proclaimed, "Gravity works!"

After the shock subsided, we cleared the new accident scene by placing Flaco's bones in a box. Later that week, I was left wondering what to do with the pieces, and suddenly I had a brilliant idea. What had been disastrous for Flaco would be fortunate for my students and me.

I disassembled Flaco's bones and placed an assortment of bones into colorful gift bags. In each bag of bones, I placed word slips with key vocabulary terms printed on them. They were terms like: long bone, flat bone, hinge joint, ball-and-socket joint, scapula, tibia, etc.

When the students arrived in class the next day, I asked them to form groups of three. Each group was given a gift bag. The task was to explore the contents of the bag. They had to touch, turn, and talk about each bone in the bag. Then they were to answer the following questions: What does the bone look like? Where in the body is it? Where in the body is it connected? Based on its shape, what is its function (job) in the body? Which vocabulary term in the bag matches which bone in the bag? Why?

OMG, as the kids would say . . . what happened that day was amazing. They loved everything about the activity, and so did I. When they finished with one bag they begged to get another one. The classroom hummed with activity. Students were thinking, describing, deciding, and naming Flaco's bones and their function in his body. A new vocabulary strategy was born! Thank you, Flaco, for reminding me that we can learn from our mistakes. This was truly a serendipitous moment!

With the Flaco success story in mind, let's explore a few details about using Vocabulary in a Bag in your classroom.

Vocabulary in a Bag—Tagging Words to Objects

There are three fundamental reasons the Vocabulary-in-a-Bag strategy stimulates academic discussions and accelerates acquisition of academic vocabulary. First, the human brain loves novelty and a little surprise . . . so long as the surprise isn't too scary! In fact, humans are hardwired to attend and respond to novel events. The gift bag and the hidden objects used for Vocabulary in a Bag are novel. Second, as every teacher can attest, students thrive on touching and exploring novel objects. Using these strategies means teachers spend less time saying, "Please don't touch that," and more time encouraging tactile exploration. And, finally, the human brain evolved for the purpose of linking to other brains, and it depends on connection and communication to stay alive. In fact, communication and connecting tells the brain to be alert, helps it learn new things, and brings it pleasure. There is a good reason why telecommunications is a multi-billion dollar industry!

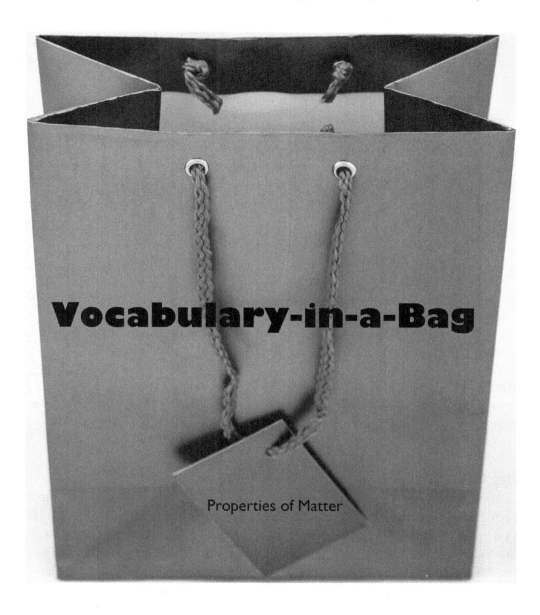

Effective communication can make life richer and people happier. When students explore the objects in a Vocabulary Bag, they automatically start connecting to content and communicating with each other. Plus the interaction makes them happy! The conversations start out as general communication and gradually become more focused as students answer questions and match objects with key terms. It is not unusual to hear students using academic vocabulary and other content-specific language as they discuss and debate.

Step-by-step teacher instructions and a sample lesson follow.

Steps and Sample Lesson

Step 1

Identify a theme or concept for the bag. All objects in the bag will be related to the theme or concept.

The concept for this sample lesson is: Properties of Matter.

Step 2

Identify seven to nine key academic vocabulary words students need to know to understand this concept.

The words for this sample lesson are: malleable, ductile, reactive, solubility, flammability, magnetic, luster, conductor, buoyant.

Step 3

In a large easy-to-read font, type one vocabulary word per line. Print the words on card stock paper for durability and cut them into individual word strips.

Step 4

Gather objects (explore the garage, junk drawer, etc.) and locate one object to represent each vocabulary term. My rule is, hunt first, shop second. If you need to buy something, never spend more than three dollars on any one object for the bag . . . think about a trip to the dollar store. Remember, the object simply needs to be connected to the vocabulary word and lead students to a better understanding of its meaning. Sometimes, when the connection between the object and the word is a bit of a stretch, it's actually more fun! Be creative and dig deep into that junk drawer(s)!

The objects for this sample lesson might be:

1. *tea candle;*
2. *piece of aluminum foil;*
3. *three shiny, fake pearl beads on a piece of string;*
4. *plastic test tube with a plastic cap containing salt and water;*

5. *three pennies taped to a folded index card (the first penny is shiny; the second penny is dull; and the last penny is corroded and greenish in appearance);*
6. *miniature plastic submarine;*
7. *small spool of copper wire;*
8. *pair of magnets;*
9. *electrical plug (one that fits into an outlet).*

Step 5

All of the objects (no word strips) are placed into the bag. You will need four bags for a class of 24 students.

Step 6

Place students into groups of four to six, and give each group a bag. Instruct students to remove the items **one at a time**. The objects should be passed around to each group member. As each student receives the object, they will comment on it. Provide the following stems for students to use when they respond:

- ◆ It looks like . . .
- ◆ It reminds me of . . .
- ◆ One thing I know about this object is . . .
- ◆ This object can be used for . . .
- ◆ One observation I can make about this object is . . .
- ◆ If I were naming this object, I would call it a . . .

Student responses for this sample lesson might include:
- ◆ *One thing I know about this object is that it is attracted to these magnets.*
- ◆ *One observation I can make about this object is that it is shiny.*

Important note: In addition to using the stems, allow time for free conversation about the objects. You want students talking, describing, and sharing thoughts and ideas.

After an object has made its way around the group, a name for it is decided on. The process continues until all objects have been described, named, and listed.

Step 7

Next, students request a copy of the word strips from the teacher. Groups discuss the words (they can use resources to investigate meanings, if needed), and attempt to match each object with its companion vocabulary word. After making the matches, they record their thinking by completing the stems in writing.

I think the (name object) might represent the word (insert vocabulary word) because (explain their thinking) . . .

Student written responses for this sample lesson might be: I think the aluminum foil might match the word malleable because it can be hammered into a thin sheet and can easily change shape.

Step 8

After all the matches are complete, students must attempt to identify the overall concept that the objects represent. They should ask themselves: What do all these objects have in common? How do the objects and the words relate to what we are learning?

Follow-up Activities

After following these steps, students can do and learn so many different things using the Vocabulary Bags . . . it's almost limitless. But here are a few of my favorite follow-up activities and ideas.

1. Randomly lay the objects and word strips out in a place where they are clearly visible to all students (under the Elmo works). Ask student volunteers to come up and collect one of the objects and its corresponding vocabulary word strip. Have the volunteers stand in front of the room. Continue until all objects and most word strips have been selected. If a student picks up an object but does not see the word strip they are looking for (someone else has picked it up already) they just take the object and get in line with the other students. Each student, in turn, will use the following stem to explain their matches:

   I think that (names object and holds it up) might match the word (says vocabulary term and holds up word strip) because . . .

   A student with an object but no word strip might say:

   I think that (names object and holds it up) might match the word (says vocabulary term) because . . . but someone else already picked it up.

As the activity progresses, students are encouraged and permitted to exchange word strips if need be. In the end, the audience gives the students who are standing a thumbs *up* if they think all matches are correct, or they can give them a thumbs *down* and proceed to offer suggestions. The teacher makes the final determination.

It is important to allow students to explore and explain different connections. Frequently, students will see and make connections the teacher might not have considered. Encourage thinking outside the box.

2. Write a list of seven to nine vocabulary words on the board. Remember, the words should be related to a single concept. Have each student select a vocabulary word and write it down. Ask them to search for an object at home that could represent the word and bring it to school. Don't be shy about listing difficult, somewhat abstract words. A student once selected the term *expeditious*. After researching its meaning, this idea evolved: an envelope containing a lengthy email followed by short tweet from Twitter, complete with #. Do you see the connection? I think you would agree that a tweet is more expeditious than an email, right? Never underestimate the creativity of your students!

3. Hang the Vocabulary Bags on the word wall. Here, students can explore them and practice matching words and objects.

4. Use the Vocabulary Bags for academic interventions, quick assessments, and/or at learning centers.

5. Have students list alternative words that match the objects in the bag.

Now let your imagination run wild. What else will you do with these Vocabulary Bags?

Curious about the correct matches for the sample lesson? Here they are:

1. *tea candle—flammability;*
2. *piece of aluminum foil—malleable;*
3. *three shiny, fake pearl beads on a piece of string—luster;*
4. *plastic test tube with a plastic cap containing salt and water—solubility;*
5. *three pennies taped to a folded index card (the first penny is shiny; the second penny is dull; and the last penny is corroded and greenish in appearance)—reactive;*

6. *miniature plastic submarine—buoyant;*
7. *small spool of copper wire—ductile;*
8. *pair of magnets—magnetic;*
9. *electrical plug (one that fits into an outlet)—conductor.*

What Research Has to Say

Two decades of research confirm that many students who struggle in school are tactile or kinesthetic learners. These students acquire and retain knowledge or skills best when they touch, feel, and experience concrete objects or engage in real-life activities.

Most of the school population excels through kinesthetic means: touching, feeling, or experiencing the material at hand. Children enter kindergarten as kinesthetic and tactual learners, moving and touching everything as they learn. By second or third grade, some students have become visual learners. During the late elementary years some students—primarily females—become auditory learners. Yet, many adults—especially males—maintain kinesthetic and tactual strengths throughout their lives.

(Stafford & Dunn, 1993)

The conclusion: object-based learning strategies, such as Vocabulary in a Bag, which allow students to touch, observe, and discuss physical objects facilitate learning for all students, particularly for those who are poor auditory learners.

Picture Pages—Using Images to Support Learning

Have you ever watched a child flip through the pages of a picture book and listened as they created their own story? Studying the images, they determine the setting, identify the characters, and decide the plot. They read the characters' emotions in their facial expressions and sort out relationships by character interactions. While picture books often appear simple, the storyline they deliver can be sophisticated, even complex. Take away the pictures and leave only the text, and much of the richness and enjoyment in the story is instantly lost. But pictures do more than make text fun and enjoyable. They provide a framework for understanding, allowing the reader to comprehend text using a creative right-brained approach.

Images activate visual centers of the brain along with multiple other areas, collectively setting imaginations free and triggering associations.

In addition, the images we view are encoded and stored in *visual long-term memory*. Research demonstrates visual memory is a massive storehouse for information and details. In one study (Brady, Konkle, Alvarez, & Oliva, 2008), participants could remember details about thousands of images after a single, short viewing. The goal of *Picture Pages* is to capitalize on the brain's massive storage capacity for visual details. As students engage in this visualization process, they can absorb large amounts of information in a short period of time . . . information that can be easily retrieved when needed.

To prepare for the *Picture Page* activity, the teacher selects a fairly difficult text that students will be required to read. Before students read the text, the teacher scans it for the purpose of creating a word list—selecting words that are fundamental to understanding the text. When the text and the words are selected, the following steps will serve as a key vocabulary strategy that can be used over and over again.

Step 1

Select a visual representation of each word on the word list. Pictures can be found, almost effortlessly, by doing an image search online.

Step 2

Create a *Picture Page* with ten to twelve thumbnail images, one image for each word selected.

Step 3

Write a numbered list of all the words the pictures represent, just below the images.

Step 4

Provide a *Picture Page* to small groups of students. The task now is for students to talk about the pictures. For example, if there is a picture of a swan, students might say, "I know that swans mate for life."

Note: Instinctually, and without asking, students will gravitate towards the list of words at the bottom of the *Picture Page* when they begin to describe each word. Quite naturally, they make a connection between the visual and the word. When they do, it strengthens the visual image with the actual word. As students make connections between words and pictures, ask them to write the number of each word beneath its picture.

DID YOU KNOW? . . .

Pictures can be used as prompts to inspire student writing. While observing and discussing a picture, ask students to do one or more of the following:

1. Make a personal connection to the picture using the sentence stem, "This picture reminds me of . . ."
2. Write a question(s) that the picture brings to mind using the sentence stem, "One question I have after observing this picture is . . ."
3. Write detailed observations of the picture.
4. Create a caption for the picture.
5. Make a list of words they associate with the picture.

Step 5

Give students a Word Journal with three columns: *Word, Your Definition, New Information* (see a copy of the Word Journal in Appendix B). Have students write all of the words from the *Picture Page* in the first column. Then, have them try their hand at writing a definition for each word . . . based on the "descriptive chatter" from their groups.

Step 6

Give students a copy of the text selected at the beginning of this activity, and have them highlight all the words from the *Picture Page*. Tell students they can make annotated notes next to the words . . . sometimes called "brain jots." For example, *agility* means jumping high.

Step 7

Have students read the passage they have been given. As they read, ask them to make notes in the last column—*New Information*—when they uncover and discover new ideas about each word from the text.

Step 8

Assess student knowledge by having students use as many words from the *Picture Page* as possible in an original piece of writing. The progression in this activity goes from images to definitions to text to writing. The process is a natural way for students to make words real!

Frequently Asked Questions

What is the Fair Use Doctrine?

The Fair Use Doctrine is a legal policy stating that portions of copyrighted materials may be used without permission of the copyright owner provided:

◆ the use is fair and reasonable;
◆ it does not substantially impair the value of the material;
◆ it does not curtail the profits reasonably expected by the owner.

Does the Fair Use Doctrine allow teachers to use images from the web for instruction without violating copyright?

To determine if the Fair Use Doctrine applies in the classroom, ask yourself this question: Why am I using this image? If the answer is for: criticism, comment, teaching (including multiple copies for classroom use), scholarship, or research, you are most likely covered by the Fair Use Doctrine.

What are public domain images and where do I find them?

Public domain images are images not restricted by copyright. You do not need a license or permission, and you are not required to pay a fee when using images in the public domain. Public domain status allows the user unrestricted access to use, copy, and alter the images, so you can be creative!

Works in the public domain include:

◆ works that automatically enter the public domain because they cannot be copyrighted, such as names, slogans, and familiar symbols;

◆ ideas and facts;

◆ processes and systems;

◆ government works, images, and documents;

◆ works that have been placed into the public domain by their creators;

◆ works that have entered the public domain because the copyright has expired.

It is highly recommended that teachers use public domain resources whenever possible. As noted, materials created by the federal government are all in the public domain, and many public agencies (National Aeronautics and Space Administration, National Parks Service, National Oceanic and Atmospheric Administration, etc.) have created educational materials that include a treasure-trove of images.

In addition, a quick internet search will provide a long list of resources for free images, as well as inexpensive stock images for purchase. Just remember, when in doubt about the fair use of an image, ask permission . . . and teach your students to do the same!

Tips for ELLs

✓ Allow ELLs to use native language dictionaries and resources as needed.

✓ Allow beginning ELL speakers to describe the objects in the Vocabulary Bag or pictures on the *Picture Pages* in their native language, but encourage them to use English words when possible.

✓ Provide ELLs with a written copy of the sentence stems used to support speaking in complete sentences.

✓ Ask ELLs to match objects to word strips in the Vocabulary Bag or pictures on the *Picture Page* with vocabulary terms in order to assess understanding (formative assessment).

✓ Allow ELLs to share native language vocabulary translations with their group members.

4

Emblematic and Iconic Gestures

Using Gestures to Build Word and Content Knowledge

Drama teachers and their students have long understood the value of moving the body, hands, or head to express meaning and thought. If an actor wants to demonstrate they are listening, a mere tilt of the head to one side or a stroke of the chin with one hand speaks volumes.

Now, neuroscience and educational research suggest significant value in incorporating gestures during instruction. The consensus is that when teachers incorporate gestures while teaching, they become more effective in three fundamental aspects:

◆ First, gesturing improves communication.
◆ Second, gesturing improves a teacher's ability to assess student knowledge.
◆ Third, gesturing has the ability to instill a profound understanding of abstract concepts in difficult content areas such as English language arts, mathematics, and science.

Here is a simple question to consider. If gesturing is proven to enhance teacher effectiveness, accelerate acquisition of academic vocabulary, increase longevity of word knowledge, and improve content comprehension, why is it absent from most classroom instruction?

One reason is that teachers need multiple concrete examples and techniques for using gestures within specific content areas. With a little imagination, teacher collaboration, and student input, gestures can be developed and used consistently. The question teachers need to ask themselves is: What could I do with my body, hands, or face that would help my students better understand a new word or a difficult concept? The gesture might be as simple as pointing to a word wall or an object. Or, it could be as elaborate as performing a skit or dramatization.

It is refreshing to hear students say, "Oh, now I see what you mean," or "Now, I remember what that is," after witnessing a simple gesture. Those comments underscore the value of gesturing. Incorporating gestures requires pre-planning and thoughtfulness, but it doesn't generate more papers to grade!

This chapter allows teachers the chance to examine effective strategies and concrete examples for using gestures in the classroom. As a result, teacher effectiveness and student performance are elevated.

Using Emblematic Gestures to Improve Communication

Teacher Journal

Talking with my Hands

Picture this . . . my students are working in small groups discussing and answering questions when I interrupt them to say: "Please stop and look up. I see and hear lots of good work going on in our classroom, but I need everyone's attention for our next step. It's a really simple one, and it's just a matter of timing and taking turns. Listen closely. After you have had a moment to talk to your partners, give them a chance to share their information too. Take time to listen to them . . . really listen. There's an old saying that I remember and can share with you. In it, it says that we have two ears and one mouth so we ought to listen twice as much as we speak. Yes, I know that talking is important because we need to verbalize our thoughts and ideas, but listening is equally important because we need to hear our partner's point of view. So as you follow this next crucial step . . . listening to your partner . . . think and reflect on all you have learned during this time. Not only do you have the knowledge you have uncovered personally, but you have more facts and viewpoints from your partner. With twice the information you originally had, you can begin your final responses."

After making my request, I looked around the room. Most students initially looked up, but many had stopped listening by the time I said, "I need everyone's attention." I was left wondering . . . what could I do differently to ensure students would listen, understand, and follow my instructions? Repeating directions over and over again wasn't making anyone in the room happy!

ELLs, particularly beginning speakers, often have difficulty understanding instructions. Students with attention problems might look up initially, hear the first few words, and then lose focus before the full message is conveyed. Both teachers and students experience confusion and frustration when instructions are not heard, understood, or followed. If, however, the teacher combines the request with simple gestures, three positive things are likely to occur. First, ELLs will comprehend the request, quickly learning new words with little difficulty. Second, the gestures are more likely to capture and hold the attention of all students because, now, students can see and hear the teacher's request. Third, incorporating gestures encodes student memory—increasing the likelihood that the teacher's request will be followed and remembered. In addition, if another reminder is needed, it can be made with a simple gesture instead of a verbal command.

Table 4.1 provides a partial list of gestures that can be used to improve communication in the classroom. These types of gestures, commonly referred to as *emblematic gestures*, can be combined with speech for more effective communication. Emblematic gestures generally have three characteristics:

◆ They are known by almost everyone in a social group or cohort.
◆ They have a direct verbal translation.
◆ Most individuals respond to them in a consistent manner.

When using emblematic gestures to communicate, teachers must be aware of and sensitive to cultural differences. Gestures can have dramatically different connotations in different cultures. For example, in the United States, the thumbs-up gesture means *all right, good job,* or *I agree*, but in other countries, the thumbs-up gesture can be insulting and offensive. It is always important to be aware and sensitive to students' unique cultural differences. In any case, teachers can still take advantage of the fact that many gestures are used worldwide and can be safely incorporated during instruction.

As an added bonus, once students see and learn gestures, they can use them to communicate with the teacher and other students in the classroom.

Table 4.1 Emblematic Gestures

Teacher Gesture	Meanings
Thumbs up	Good job, I agree. You are correct. All right. (Note: In some cultures, these gestures can have a negative or offensive connotation.)
Thumb up, wiggling back and forth	Almost right. On the right track. Not sure. (This gesture implies that the speaker should keep thinking.)
Thumbs down	Poor job. I disagree. You are off course.
Hand lifted with palm facing away, aka the stop sign	Please stop. Reconsider what you are doing or thinking.
Hands extended moving up and down slightly with palms facing the floor	Slow down. Be careful.
Index finger on one hand is extended and placed vertically in front of the lips	Shush. Stop talking. Be quiet.
Index finger placed over lips with a shoulder shrug and eyes cast upward . . . looks like a thinking statue	Let me think about that.
Index finger and thumb form a circle with three remaining fingers extended	OK. That's good. That works for me.
Fingers are kept straight and together while moving up and down and tapping the thumb below the "talking hand"	Start talking. Keep talking.
The talking hand is followed by a fist drawn towards the heart	You must verbalize "talk" in order to internalize thoughts and concepts.
Hand rubbing	Indicates that one feels cold. Shows that one is expecting or anticipating something exciting or surprising to take place.
Lowering the torso or head slightly, as in a bow	This is a show of respect in many cultures.
Elbow or fist bump	Shows approval. Sometimes used as a greeting.
Eye roll, rotating the eyes upward and back down	Indicates contempt, boredom, frustration, or exasperation.
Head bobble up and down	This is an affirmative response or acknowledgment.
Head or index finger shaking side to side	No, no. Disapproval.
Shoulder shrug—lifting both shoulders up . . . sometimes accompanied by palms up, bent elbows, and raised eyebrows	Lifting both shoulders indicates lack of knowledge or concern.
A melodramatic gesture made by lifting the arm and placing the back of the hand on the forehead	Distress. I can't believe I just did that. Someone has received bad news.

Let's take a minute and revisit the teacher instructions (in Teacher Journal: Talking with my Hands) used as an example at the start of this chapter. The instructions start with, *Please stop and look up . . .*

Then, review the list of emblematic gestures in Table 4.1. How could a teacher use gestures to communicate the request and know that all students will understand?

Now rub your hands together and get ready to practice using emblematic gestures to communicate your response!

Using Iconic Gestures to Build Word and Content Knowledge

Teacher Journal

The Clock Was Ticking

Melinda was twelve years old when we met, and a student in my seventh-grade science class. Like many students at our school, Melinda was an English Language Learner and a beginning speaker. It was obvious that she had difficulty understanding content delivered verbally and struggled sharing her thoughts and knowledge with other students. I used pictures to illustrate simple words and ideas, but she continued to struggle with complex science content. It was also obvious that if Melinda was going to master speaking English, she needed more opportunities to practice speaking English! Beginning speakers need a safe structured environment to practice their skills. Modeling, guidance, and repetition are essential. The challenge is to unravel the complexity of science by making it comprehensible. In addition, I needed to ensure that students like Melinda acquired the content knowledge and language skills they needed to succeed. The clock was ticking. If gaps in Melinda's vocabulary persisted, she would have struggled with speaking, reading, and writing. In addition, her self-confidence would be low, and she would most likely fail in school. Determined to accelerate Melinda's word knowledge and prevent her from being a long-term "ELL," I started using a new teaching strategy. Students called it "talking with your hands."

As I held up my two hands and drew them into the shape of the letter "W," Melinda's face lit up! She knew that this was going to be a lesson she could comprehend. She followed my lead step-by-step, imitating my gestures and repeating my words with confidence. In fact, all of the students engaged immediately. It was time to have some fun!

Talking with my Hands—A Model Lesson Using Iconic Gestures

The following earth science lesson is a difficult one: helping students discern the difference between four (frequently confused) geological processes/terms: *weathering, sediment, erosion,* and *deposition.*

Not only is it a difficult lesson to deliver to English-speaking students, it is doubly difficult for ELLs. Ideally, rocks, gravel, sand, water, wind, and a stream table are needed to model these processes. Teachers, however, frequently do not teach in an ideal world. Without a stream table or access to other materials, an effective teaching strategy is the best way forward. By design, the lesson would be:

◆ comprehensible to all students, especially ELLs and special education students;
◆ language-rich to build academic vocabulary skills;
◆ quick, concise, and easy to implement;
◆ tactile, engaging, and repeatable;
◆ encoded in long-term memory . . . to reduce errors when students recall the information.

The images and text that follow demonstrate how gestures, in combination with succinct verbiage (rich in academic vocabulary), can accomplish the objectives listed above. Unlike standalone emblematic gestures, such as a "head nod" or a "finger wag," the gestures used in this lesson are specifically designed to accompany speech, not replace it. Sometimes referred to as *iconic gestures* or *illustrators,* these movements are synchronized with speech and are meant to add detail, clarity, and mental imagery to the conversation.

The sample lesson, seen below, is so simple, so powerful, and so easy to repeat. And, it is highly effective at making the content comprehensible and perfect for encoding long-term memory. It demonstrates how iconic gestures matched with academic language can build word knowledge and content knowledge quickly and effectively. As an added bonus . . . it's really fun!

To start, make the shape of the letter "W" with the hands. This signals a lesson that students can recognize because they can all understand gestures. All they have to do is follow the lead . . . step by step, imitating gestures and repeating words. In the process, their confidence grows.

Sample Lesson Using Gesturing

Model the hand gestures in the sequence below and ask students to copy the gestures. Next, provide the text and ask students to repeat what they hear.

Step 1

"W" stands for the term **weathering**. Notice the **"ing"** at the end of the word weather**ing** (emphasize **ing**), not *weather* (shake finger as if to say "no"), not like a rainy day (make rain motion with fingers) or a sunny day (place arms in a circular position overhead to represent the sun). Have students repeat: the "W" stands for **weathering.**

Figure 4.1

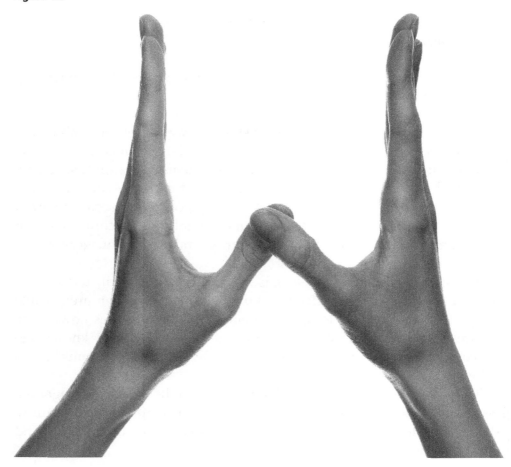

Step 2

Crack the "W" apart making a breaking sound. Form a cup with two hands and say: **weathering** is when big rocks break apart and become smaller and smaller rocks. The small rocks might appear as sand or dirt. This weathered material is called **sediment**. Can you say that for me? **Sediment**. Pretend the sediment is in your hands (move cupped hands forward and shake). **Sediment** is the result of rocks weathering. It is when big rocks break down into smaller rocks (repeat gesture for **weathering** as in Step 1). Typically, **sediment** does not (shake finger back and forth) stay in one place. Instead it moves (move cupped hands from side to side). Take a minute and show your partner one way you could get the **sediment** in your hands to move (students model with partners).

Figure 4.2

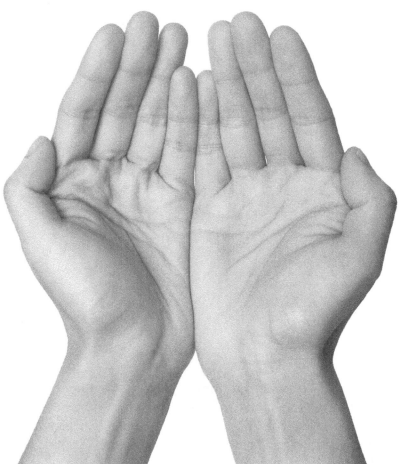

Step 3

Many of you did this (teacher gestures and pretends to blow the sediment out on their hands). You are right, wind can move sediment, and it looks like a sandstorm!

Figure 4.3

Step 4

Some of you did this (teacher gestures separating the fingers as if to let the sediment sift through the hands and fall to the ground). You are right; gravity can move sediment from higher elevations to lower elevations (model high and low with hands). It looks like a landslide! (Gesture by showing hands moving quickly down a steep incline.)

Figure 4.4

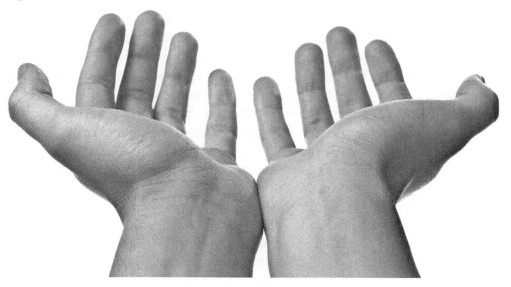

Step 5

Here's a movement I didn't see (teacher makes a wave motion, moving the hand up and down). What else can move **sediment**? That's right, water can move sediment from one place to another. When sediment moves from one place to another by wind action (blow into hands), gravity (open fingers), or water (make wave motion), it is called **erosion**. Repeat this new word, **erosion**. Now, turn to your partners and show them three factors in the environment that can cause **erosion** of sediment. (Students make gestures for wind, gravity, and water.)

Figure 4.5

Step 6

As sediment moves, erosion takes place. Then, the sediment eventually loses energy (bend arms to make bicep muscles) and stops moving. The sediment settles to the ground (model energy loss) when the wind stops blowing, when it reaches the bottom of the hill, or when water in a stream slows down. We call this **deposition**. Repeat the new word, **deposition**. Deposition is when sediment stops moving, settles to the ground (use index finger to point towards the ground), and accumulates (use hands to show layers/ stacks of sediment on the ground).

Simple hand gestures in combination with the text for this earth science lesson dramatically increases student engagement, understanding, and retention of content. The gestures and dialogue can be easily repeated by the teacher to review, or can be modeled by the student to demonstrate mastery. It's fun, quick, and highly effective for all students!

Take note, however, that when students first experience gesturing, they may wonder what the teacher is doing with her hands. One student was overheard saying to a newcomer, "Oh, Mrs. B teaches us new things using her hands and gestures sometimes. Last week she taught us about the phases of the moon. You won't believe how she acted out waxing and waning and

Figure 4.6

the difference between a *full moon* and a *new moon*. She turned her back, bent downward at the waist and pretended to "moon" us. As she moved her hands from her waist to her knees and back to her waist, she told us: when the moon is waxing, it is headed towards a full moon. This means the entire lighted surface of the moon is visible from Earth. When the moon is waning, it is headed towards a new moon, and no moon appears in the nighttime sky. We repeated the gestures and explanations over and over. At first we couldn't stop laughing. But we also couldn't forget what waxing and waning meant or what a full moon and new moon looks like! Trust me, she's really good at this. It makes things easy to understand and remember."

When spontaneous and heartwarming compliments like this happen, teaching becomes so rewarding. When gesturing is used in the classroom, students "get it" and "remember it" in a way they often do not using standard direct instruction. The outcomes and benefits are immeasurable. Gestures definitely lend a hand to learning!

Frequently Asked Questions

Where can I find good ideas for using gestures in my specific content-area?

The key to finding and developing engaging and effective gestures is teacher collaboration. Teachers need to share their ideas. Set aside time during regular department planning to share ideas about how to incorporate gestures into instruction. As a team, be committed to using gestures whenever possible. I am always amazed at the creativity of teachers when it comes to lesson design. But what is equally amazing is the potential for creative expression in their students. Some of the best gestures are developed by students for other students. Don't be afraid to give students a list of difficult-to-learn words or a challenging concept and ask them to write the lesson dialogue and develop the corresponding gestures. And finally, a quick internet search can uncover some real gems. I did a quick internet search using "ideas for teaching math with hand gestures," and it produced a plethora of great ideas!

DID YOU KNOW? . . .

Total physical response (TPR) is a language teaching method developed by James Asher, a professor emeritus of psychology at San José

State University. TPR is based on the *coordination of language and physical movement*. In a stress-free environment, the language learner's primary role is to listen to the teacher's command and perform a series of actions based on the command. The teacher provides the dialogue, acting as a director of the "stage play" in which the students are the actors.

Using TPR students acquire new English vocabulary by listening to and carrying out spoken instructions. In this early phase of language learning, students are not required to speak. The teacher models the commands and repeats and reviews them until the students can perform them with no difficulty. This language teaching method, developed over four decades ago, continues to be a cornerstone strategy for beginning speakers as they learn a new language. Dr. Asher suggests that students can learn between 12 and 36 words for every hour of instruction, depending on their language level and class size (Asher, 2009).

How often should students repeat gestures?

Repeated practice builds stronger connections between neurons in the brain. When gestures are performed and linked to information verbally stated, new connections between neurons in the brain are established. If I form my hands in the shape of the letter "W," my students automatically make the "cracking apart" sound and the word "weathering" flashes in their minds. When I cup my hands and ask them "What am I holding?" they shout "sediment." Neuroscientists like to say, practice does not necessarily make perfect but it does make permanent! Keep repeating until the gesture and the information are permanently linked.

Are gestures appropriate for high school students or will they be perceived as too elementary?

Some high school teachers are reluctant to uses gestures for this reason. Some teachers might feel that they "aren't the drama type." Yet, I consistently hear that students are increasingly disengaged, bored, or disconnected, or that students struggle with complex concepts and long-term retention. Gesturing can be an effective solution to tackle these problems. If you aren't comfortable with gesturing, ask for student volunteers to help. Involving secondary students in the process is very important. After I teach a gesture, I will get students to lead the class for repeated practice. Many students love to "take the stage" and demonstrate knowledge.

Can student-generated gestures be used to assess knowledge?

Absolutely! Gestures that students produce related to a task have been shown to reflect their knowledge of the task, particularly at moments of transition. Student-generated gestures can uncover misconceptions, confusion in thinking, or gaps in understanding. Several studies suggest that the gestures students produce while speaking reveal much more about what they are thinking than their speech alone (Goldin-Meadow, 2000).

What Research Has To Say

Cognitive scientist Susan Cook and her colleagues performed an experiment on gestures used during a mathematics lesson (Cook, Mitchell, & Goldin-Meadow, 2008). Students in grades three and four were given math problems. For example:

$$4 + 3 = \underline{\quad} + 6$$

The task was to find the number that would make both sides of the equation equal. When presented with the task none of the students were able to solve these problems on their own.

Next, the teacher-provided instructions were administered in three different formats: one using speech, a second using gestures, and the third using speech plus gestures. After each student received instruction in just one of these methods, they were given a new problem. The instructor told the students to solve the problem using the method they had practiced. Students in all three groups improved their performance. But something fascinating surfaced when the students were retested four weeks later. Students who had improved using gestures, either alone or paired with speech, were more likely to have maintained their improvement four weeks later. These students were prone to remember the strategy and transfer it to new problems. Two conclusions were drawn:

1. Pairing gestures with speech for math instruction resulted in improved understanding, better recall, and improved ability to transfer skills to a new problem.
2. Merely *watching* gestures can help students learn and recall information.

Tips to Consider for ELLs

✓ When combining speech with gestures, provide the dialogue in writing. Consider using images in the background to support understanding. This provides both visual and auditory support as ELLs learn new words and concepts.

✓ Provide multiple opportunities for practice and monitor pronunciation.

✓ Be sensitive to cultural differences. Gestures appropriate in one culture might be offensive in another.

✓ Use gestures as one method of assessing student knowledge.

✓ Teach gestures to ELLs and encourage their use of gestures to improve communication with teachers and other students.

PART II
Structured Opportunities for Using Academic Vocabulary

5

Numbered Heads and Scaffolded Questions

Can You See Me . . . Can You Hear Me?

After weeks of classroom observations at a local middle school, one common practice stood out: When teachers asked a question, I could predict with a high degree of accuracy which students would likely not provide the answer. Many, in fact, most teachers I observed were very reluctant to call on their ELL students to share their ideas verbally with the class. Curious about why teachers were so apprehensive about calling on ELLs, I asked them. In fact, I asked hundreds of teachers, "Why do you think teachers are frequently reluctant to call on ELL students to share their ideas?" Here is a partial list of teacher responses.

I think teachers are reluctant to call on ELL students because . . .

1. Their language skills are weak, and they don't want to embarrass them.
2. It can take a long time for ELLs to compose a response, and it wastes a lot of class time.
3. They might not understand the question.
4. They do not volunteer answers, and other students do raise their hands to respond.
5. They are less likely to provide a high-quality answer.
6. They get upset if I ask them to speak on the spur of the moment in front of their classmates.

7. Teachers frequently have to coach ELLs as they answer, and this causes other students to become bored and lose focus.
8. ELLs generally don't want to be called on.

Next, I asked ELLs why they thought their teachers might be reluctant to call on them. Here's what ELL students had to share.

I think my teachers are reluctant to call on me (an ELL student) because...

1. I am quiet and shy so they don't really notice me in class.
2. They know other students have better answers so they call on them first.
3. They mostly call on smart students.
4. They call on students who are not paying attention in class, and I usually listen during class.
5. I don't raise my hand to answer like other students do.
6. They know I struggle with English (have an accent), and other students probably won't understand me.
7. They think other students might make fun of the way I speak.

No matter what the reason, the reality of not calling on ELLs delays their progress significantly as they try to acquire English skills. Even shy, English-speaking students are penalized. A randomized system for calling on students is desperately needed . . . one that eliminates their "reasons" for not calling on certain students. This system tells all students that their thoughts and opinions are valuable. In the words of one ELL student, "I want my teacher to see me and hear me. It's hard sitting quiet all day and not talking. I know I'm never going to learn English if I don't start using it."

The strategy needed is Numbered Heads paired with Scaffolded Questions: With this system in place . . . class participation skyrockets!

Verbalize to Internalize—Getting Students to Use Academic Vocabulary When Speaking

Have you ever "talked" your way through a problem? Have you ever attended a book study and discovered that talking with others about the book significantly changed or deepened your understanding of the story?

In the classroom, just like in a book study, talking about content provides clarity and deepens understanding. However, most teachers would agree that getting students to talk about content is difficult. In particular, it is difficult to get students to talk about content using *academic vocabulary*. When asked specific content-related questions, students often provide a "dumbed down" response, that is, a response void of core academic vocabulary. Here's an example:

Teacher–Student Dialogue

Teacher: Last year you learned about plants and photosynthesis. Can anyone tell me what they recall about photosynthesis?

Student: I remember. It's when plants use the sun to make food. They use these green things in their cells to make this sugary stuff.

While the student response demonstrates a basic understanding of the term *photosynthesis*, it does not incorporate the use of any key academic terms associated with the concept. Students often find it difficult to find the right words to explain their answers, and they have difficulty constructing complex, language-rich sentences. Using a technique called Numbered Heads plus Scaffolded Questions provides support for all students as they practice using academic vocabulary in complete sentences.

Raise Your Hand If You Have a Question

Thinking is driven by questions . . . not answers. Questions stir neural networks, activate prior knowledge, and motivate the brain to explore new ideas. Conversely, answers act as stop signs; they quiet the thinking process.

Answers are best followed by more questions. Learning takes place when we question what we learn, not when we answer questions. As strange as it sounds, a good answer is best assimilated when followed by another question! Encourage students to ask questions, and reinforce the fact that answers take shape and form as the next question is asked. Ask students to recall how they used to ask "why" repeatedly when they were younger. Tell them that the answer to the "why" question helped them understand the answer better. The proverbial, "Why is the sky blue?" is a perfect example. This question/answer methodology happens in all stages of life, even for adults.

Sometimes when teachers ask questions, thinking doesn't always happen. Consider the following scenarios. The teacher asks a question, and . . .

1. A consistent, limited number of higher performing students raise their hands to answer.
2. No students offer an answer so the teacher answers the question.

3. A student offers an incorrect answer that must be corrected by the teacher or another student.
4. The teacher cold-calls a student who has not been participating or paying attention, and the student responds with, "I don't know."

When these predictable responses occur, questions seem to interrupt teacher instruction, and students begin to "check out" of the learning process. They know that a handful of students will provide the answers. The result is that many minds in the classroom are essentially lost in the learning process. They drift in and out of the conversation, or they completely shut down. At best, students are passively listening because they know little is expected of them to think, produce, or share answers with others in class. At this point, participation is limited and interest is low.

Creating an environment where all students are actively thinking about the question posed by the teacher means that structured, safe opportunities for sharing ideas and thoughts are built into the classroom procedure. To do this effectively can be challenging, but rewarding. Once it is established, students are well-grounded in a routine that works to their benefit. It means there is a system in place, a protocol that provides frequent opportunities for all students to participate in the learning process, without derailing the lesson. The key is to structure an environment where students believe that each question is intended for them. This creates an expectant atmosphere where students can actively think about the question, prepare an answer, and share their thoughts with the class. Under these circumstances, engagement and participation are significantly elevated.

Ask yourself the following questions about your classroom environment:*

◆ Do you have a system for asking and answering questions?
◆ Does it imply that you value student input and ideas?
◆ Do all students understand teacher expectations?
◆ Do students understand that everyone in class is responsible for thinking, sharing, and participating?
◆ Do all students know they can learn by participating?

* Reflecting on these questions will provide insight about your classroom environment.

If any responses to these questions seem vague or perplexing, an explanation of the Numbered Heads strategy will help put this into perspective. While this strategy may sound like the Think-Pair-Share activity—a good one in certain instances—Numbered Heads requires more steps and is more advanced.

The protocol in this strategy ensures that teachers ask frequent high-quality questions and that all students engage in thinking, sharing, and learning.

To start Numbered Heads, pose a relevant, engaging question to the class approximately every fifteen minutes. Then, ask students to contemplate a response to the question by gathering information from others. Based on the information students have uncovered in the information-gathering process, ask them to share their ideas in complete sentences using core academic language.

Here's how it works!

Figure 5.1

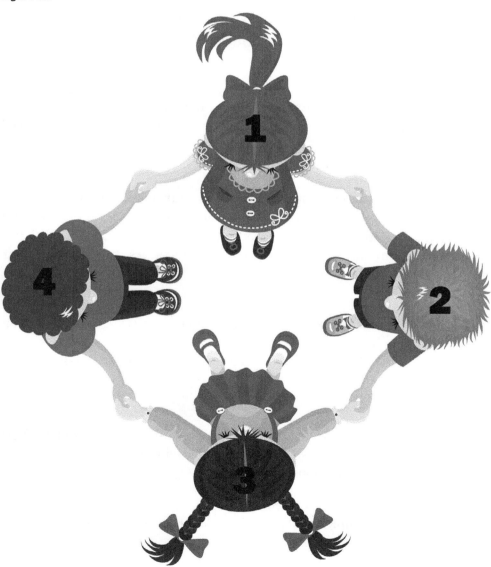

Numbered Heads and Scaffolded Questions

Students in class are assigned a number from 1 to 4 (see Figure 5.1). Permanent numbers can be taped on desks to make the process easy for everyday use. However, if students rotate or change seats, their number changes.

Step 1
Periodically, the teacher stops and says, "I have a question for you. I was wondering . . ." The question is stated aloud and written (posted) in the classroom for students to read.

A sample question might be: What picture comes to mind when you think about *animal adaptations*?

Step 2
After the question is stated and posted in the classroom, the teacher provides a written sentence stem/sentence starter for the question.

A sample sentence stem would be: When I think about the word *animal adaptations,* I picture . . .

Step 3
Students think about the question and formulate an answer in their minds or write the answer on paper. Students share their response with one or more partner/s, practicing (speaking or reading) their response. They MUST use the sentence stem and speak in complete sentences. As they listen to their partner/s, they gather more information.

Sample responses would be:

Student A: When I think about *animal adaptations,* I picture a giraffe with a long neck.

Student B: When I think about *animal adaptations,* I picture a peacock's fancy tail feathers.

Step 4
Students return to their seats (if they have been standing) or return their attention to the teacher after sharing and gathering information. The teacher models an appropriate response.

A sample response would be:

Teacher: When I think about *animal adaptations,* I picture the hooves on a horse or a cow.

Step 5

The teacher randomly selects a number from 1 to 4 and asks students with that number to stand. One by one, students respond to the question, using the sentence stem. After each student reads their response, they sit down.

Step 6

After all students have shared their responses, the teacher asks follow-up questions that encourage students to stretch or clarify their thoughts and ideas.

Summary of Numbered Heads

1. Pose and post the **question**.
2. Post the **sentence stem/sentence starter**.
3. Have students **gather/share information.** (This can include a written response.)
4. **Model a response** for students.
5. **Select a number** at random **and** have students **share**.
6. **Assess, stretch, and clarify**.

Remember, each step in the Numbered Heads process should be followed in step-by-step order. Omitting steps will negate many of the benefits. For example, if students are not given time to gather information, their responses may not be the high-quality responses the teacher expects. Or, if sentence stems are not provided for students to read and use, they may need the question repeated; their responses may include informal language; or their responses may not contain academic language.

Frequently Asked Questions

How often should I use the Numbered Heads strategy?

It is recommended that it be used approximately every fifteen to twenty minutes during direct instruction. Its purpose is to stop the output of information in order to assess student thinking and understanding during short intervals. Each Numbered Heads question serves as a "mini" formative assessment, allowing the teacher to randomly collect immediate feedback from multiple students. Now, the teacher has quick access to student knowledge and understanding. In addition, the teacher knows what the student is thinking. Student responses assess student learning, and instruction can be adjusted to better meet student needs. Some teachers may say that what students learn from instruction is unpredictable. Numbered Heads allows teachers to probe the thinking of all students and adapt to their needs.

What types of questions work well with the Numbered Heads strategy?

Generally, it is recommended that teachers avoid using **closed questions**, those that can be answered with a single word, short phase, or a yes/no response. Closed questions might start with words such as, *define, name, list,* or *identify.*

Instead, ask **open questions**, those that require students to *think* and *reflect.* Open questions encourage students to share their *feelings* and *opinions.* Open questions often start with words such as *what, why, how, describe, compare, predict,* or *explain.* For example, the teacher might start a unit about genetic diversity by asking the question: "What words come to mind when you hear the term *genetics*?" A sample sentence stem for students might be: "When I hear the term *genetics,* one word that comes to mind is . . ." Although the question generates a single-word response, listening to the responses can provide insight into the depth of knowledge students have. In addition, it serves as a quick and effective prior knowledge check. If words like *chromosome, DNA, mutation, crossbreeding, GMO foods,* and *cloning* are shared, the teacher can assume students have good working knowledge of the term. If, however, students complete the stem using words like *sister, brother, mother, twins,* it demonstrates a lack of experience with the term.

This type of open question can be called a *softball* question. It is designed to get students thinking, picturing, and reviewing. These questions solicit a quick response, and there is clearly no right or wrong answer. Using a softball thinking question to start Numbered Heads warms up the brain and prepares it for more complex, thought-provoking questions to follow. In fact, softball questions set the stage for listening, thinking, and learning. When first introducing the Numbered Heads system, a series of softball questions helps students become comfortable with the strategy. For many students, standing in front of their classmates and responding to questions is a scary proposition. Softball questions tell students that the teacher is interested in their thoughts, ideas, and opinions. If teachers know what students are thinking, teachers know students are learning!

Can you ask more complex questions using Numbered Heads?

Absolutely! In fact, that is the goal. While the first Numbered Heads question might be a quick and easy response for students, subsequent scaffolded questions promote more complex thinking. Scaffolded questions build one upon the other, much like scaffolding platforms support workers on the sides of a building under construction. As the scaffolds allow workers to go higher and higher, scaffolded questions require students to do the same . . . expand step-by-step to answer higher-order thinking questions. Scaffolded questions, therefore, elevate student thinking. Note: As the complexity of each question builds so does student thinking power.

Examples of three scaffolded questions and sentence stems
1. Question and Stem
   What picture comes to mind when you think about *animal adaptations*?
   When I think about *animal adaptations*, I picture . . .
2. Question and Stem
   What is one example of an animal *adaptation* that would *increase* the *likelihood* of *survival*?
   One example of an *animal adaptation* is . . . It *increases* the *likelihood* of *survival* by . . .
3. Question and Stem
   Do humans have any *unique adaptations* to improve our *survival rate*?
   One *unique adaptation* humans have is . . . which improves our *survival rate* by . . .

Note: Question #1 simply asks for a single example. Question #2 builds or scaffolds on the first question because it asks students to recall a specific example of an *animal adaptation* and to explain how it increases the likelihood of survival for the species they name in the first question. Summarily, Question #2 assumes that students have discussed or read multiple examples of *animal adaptations*. Question #3 asks students to analyze human characteristics and how they might compare to *animal adaptations*. Hierarchically, it requires students to apply their learning to a new situation. This is the object and process of a scaffolded questioning technique.

Jokingly, Question #1 can be described as blooming easy; Question #2 can be called blooming thoughtful; and Question #3 might be blooming hard. Of course, the reference is to Benjamin Bloom's taxonomy and the way it distinguishes different levels of questions in an educational setting! Figure 5.2 provides a visual summary of Bloom's taxonomy levels.

Figure 5.2

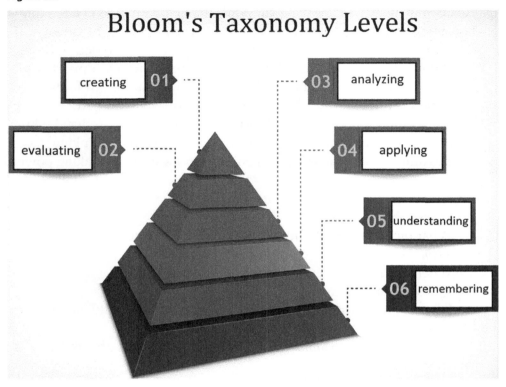

In summary, scaffolded questions and stems are leveled, increasing in complexity. Introductory questions and stems might include:

◆ What is one thing you remember about . . . ?
   One thing I remember about . . . is . . .
◆ What words do you associate with . . . ?
   Words I associate with . . . are . . .
◆ How would you describe . . . ?
   I would describe . . . as . . .

Transition questions that would require more complex thinking may be written like this:

◆ What was the most effective strategy used by your group?
   The most effective strategy our group used was . . .
◆ Which step in the math problem was the most complex?
   The most complex strategy in the math problem was . . .

◆ What is the connotation of the word . . . ?
  The connotation of the word . . . is . . .
◆ How would the changes to . . . be obvious?
  The changes to . . . would be obvious because . . .
◆ How does the text explain habitat?
  The text explains habitat by saying that it is . . .
◆ How would you determine if an atom is an isotope?
  I would determine if an atom is an isotope by analyzing . . .
◆ If cumulonimbus clouds are present in the sky, what assumptions
  might you make?
  If cumulonimbus clouds are present, I might assume . . .
◆ How does the author foreshadow events in the story?
  The author foreshadows events in the story by . . .
◆ How are fractions used in everyday life?
  Fractions are used every day when . . .

What should I do if a student does not stand and share when his/her number is called?
This is a problem that can emerge when teachers first begin to use the
Numbered Heads strategy in the classroom. Teachers need to be careful
not to single out or embarrass the student who elects not to stand. Some
students need an opportunity to see how the strategy works before they
buy into the process. Remember, once a number has been selected and students are standing, teachers can use their discretion to determine which
student shares first. Calling on students who are motivated to share their
responses allows time for more reluctant students to prepare an answer.
If students are aware of the many benefits of participating, they are more
likely to engage and cooperate. Try reassuring these students by telling
them they won't be selected to be the first one to answer. If they know
they will have an opportunity to hear three to four other students respond
first, they are more likely to participate. Generally, if a student is not participating, it is because they are fearful or nervous. Ask them about their
concerns privately and help develop a plan to ease their worries.

The following list enumerates the benefits of participating in a Numbered Heads activity. This list can be shared with students to build enthusiasm for the strategy.

1. The Numbered Heads strategy always provides an opportunity for
   students to gather information before they respond to a question.
   Students know when their number will be called; this eliminates
   nervousness, anticipation, and/or embarrassment.

2. Teachers will always post questions and sentence stems to help students form responses using complete sentences and appropriate academic language. This prevents students from asking, "What was the question?" because they already know it.

3. Students are always able to ask for information about words used in the question before they answer. For example, if the question is, "What are the **benefits** of **genetic engineering**?" students can ask the teacher to clarify the meaning of the word *benefits* or to briefly redefine *genetic engineering*. An alternative would be to direct students to a specific page in the textbook, a glossary, or individual notes to acquire the information needed to better understand and answer the question.

4. Typically, students will have an opportunity to hear other student responses before they have to answer. This is particularly important for ELL students. They can read/reread the stem and mentally practice their answer as they listen to other students respond first. This builds confidence and reinforces correct pronunciation of difficult-to-pronounce words.

5. Numbered Heads provides students with much needed practice in using academic language in oral responses. This more formal register does not come naturally to most students, and they are unlikely to acquire this skill outside the classroom. Using and practicing academic language will help students understand more complex text, e.g. textbooks and formal assessments.

6. When students write their responses and read them to partners, they become better readers and writers.

7. Being able to eloquently explain thoughts or positions gives students the power to convey information precisely. This is a huge benefit for the future. Ask students to think about a first job interview or a time when they lobbied their parents for that new smartphone!

Go ahead, be blooming creative when writing questions. Design your questions to make students think, discuss, debate, and share!

Numbered Heads with a Cooperative Learning Twist

To put a new spin on things, add a cooperative learning twist.

1. Place students into groups of four. Assign each group a letter, A, B, C, etc.

2. Have students within each group number off, 1–4.

3. Assign groups a specific task. The task can be the same for all groups or each group can be assigned varied tasks. For example, groups might be given informational text to read, a model to explore, or a math problem to solve.
4. Provide a list of scaffolded questions, related to the assigned task, to each group. Have students complete the task and collaboratively answer the scaffolded questions.
5. Provide resources for students, as needed. For example, students might use internet access to gather information or research ideas. Or, the teacher might provide teaching diagrams, models, or sample problems to support students as they work on the task.
6. Select a number from 1 to 4 after groups complete their tasks and have drafted responses to the scaffolded questions. The student with the selected number will stand and share the group response.
7. Select a group letter and number and have only one student respond if time is a factor. Other groups can comment or offer input as time allows.

The Numbered Heads strategy works well in math classrooms, as well. Many students express extreme math anxiety when asked to complete a math problem in front of the class. In addition, students working independently often get stuck and are unable to solve a math problem without support. Using Numbered Heads, students work cooperatively to solve math problems as they discuss strategies and answer scaffolded questions. Students are held individually accountable, but they experience and reap the benefits of working in a small learning community. Randomly selected individuals can go to the board to show their work or share answers to questions with confidence because they have had the support of their group members.

Sample scaffolded math questions might include:
◆ Question 1: What information is necessary to solve the problem?
   Stem 1: The information we need to solve the problem includes . . .
◆ Question 2: What steps did you take to solve this problem?
   Stem 2: To solve the problem, we took the following steps . . .
◆ Question 3: What other "real-world" problem could you solve using this math strategy?
   Stem 3: We could figure out . . . by using this strategy.

DID YOU KNOW? . . .

About 85 percent of students in introductory math classes claimed to experience some mild math anxiety (Perry, 2004). Further study revealed that math anxiety is reduced when students:

- ◆ work with a partner;
- ◆ work in cooperative learning groups;
- ◆ use manipulatives;
- ◆ write and answer questions about the problems they are solving.

6

Read, Talk, Write—Using Academic Vocabulary

As previously stated, students need multiple exposures to new words and repeated opportunities to use them in oral and written language. To accomplish this, teachers must seek out and implement effective strategies to dramatically increase student-to-student opportunities for listening, reading, talking, and writing using academic language.

Educational research consistently confirms two truths:

1. Students build word knowledge and content expertise when they engage in academic conversations.
2. Students must read deeply about a topic in order to be able to write well about it.

With these truths in mind, I recommend the following two strategies: Sentence Puzzlers and Walk, Talk, Write, and Post. Using these strategies can quickly transform a language-poor classroom into a language-rich environment. Sentence Puzzlers get students reading language-rich text with fluency and confidence. Walk, Talk, Write, and Post (and variations of it) provides valuable opportunities to encounter new words when reading and practice using new words when speaking and writing. The best way to become a better reader is to read more. And the best way to understand what we read is to talk, think, and write about it.

Let's investigate how to effectively implement Sentence Puzzlers and Walk, Talk, Write, and Post in the classroom.

Sentence Puzzlers

Teacher Journal

Reading to Learn . . .

Bethany's school experience left her feeling defeated and frustrated. Her struggles in school started in fourth grade, accelerated in middle school, and exploded in high school. When I first met her, she was a high school dropout, returning to school to get her GED. Exhausted by working long hours at dead-end jobs for a minimum wage, she was searching for more direction and a path to a better life. School and a degree, she had been told, were the answer.

Like many GED programs, Bethany's studies primarily consisted of computer-based learning. She was required to read passages, watch animations/videos, respond to questions, and ultimately pass a computer-based assessment. For Bethany, the problem was reading. Reading a text message was easy, but comprehending a complex passage about genetic inheritance was a nearly impossible task. Bethany lacked both skill and confidence when reading academic text. She was intimidated by the words and the complexity of the language. "Why don't they say what they mean?" she would complain. "Why do they always have to make it sound so complicated?" she would protest. But, she worked hard to master the skills she needed.

While she was steadily building word knowledge, she was still reluctant to read grade-level text. As her teacher, I was in search of a strategy to boost her confidence and improve her reading comprehension skills. The strategy needed to be simple and effective. It needed to involve collaboration with friends, no computers screens, and it needed to be fun.

We called the new strategy **Sentence Puzzlers**. It wasn't fancy or complicated, but it did inspire student effort, and it did provide valuable practice in reading academic text, often called "textbook talk" by the students. Here's how it works . . .

Step 1

Select a challenging reading passage, relevant to the content strand being taught, from a textbook or other resource. The passage should be rich in

TOGETHER EVERYONE ACHIEVES MORE

academic vocabulary, and it should include complex sentences with sophisticated language.

Step 2

Use the passage as a guide to copy or construct four to five sentences. Don't be afraid to write compound, complex sentences. The text should be slightly challenging, somewhat outside students' sphere of expertise, and a little above the "pay grade" of most students. The sample sentences below would be appropriate for high school biology students.

Sample sentences:

1. Located on a chromosome, a gene is a specific sequence of nucleotides in DNA or RNA that serves as the functional unit of inheritance and controls the transmission and expression of one or more traits by specifying the structure of a particular protein.
2. When viewed under a light microscope, chromosomes—composed of protein and long, coiled strands of DNA—become highly

condensed during mitotic cell division and are visible as distinct, rod, or x-shaped structures in the nucleus of cells.

3. The genetic code, determined by the sequence of nucleotides in DNA, is read and translated by a cell to produce a chain of amino acids, which in turn, folds into large biological molecules known as proteins.

4. A mutation, resulting from a change to a gene's DNA, can alter a protein's amino acid sequence, thereby changing its shape and function and rendering the protein ineffective or even malignant.

Step 3

Open a Word document on the computer and set the page margins to wide. Begin typing the selected sentences, using a large font size (recommended 65–72 point). A single sentence may span two to three pages, and it may be fragmented into eight to sixteen lines. After typing the sentences, **embolden** the content-specific *academic terms* (glossary words), and *italicize* the unfamiliar *processing words* (general utility words required for constructing sentences). Remember, do not underestimate the importance of processing words. Try reading only the **bold** words in the sentence below. Without the italicized words (the processing words), it is easy to see that it makes absolutely no sense!

> **Chromosomes**, *composed* of **protein** and long *coiled strands* of **DNA**, become highly *condensed* during **mitotic cell division** and are visible as *distinct* rod or x-shaped structures in the **nucleus** of **cells** when viewed under a **light microscope**.

Step 4

Print the Word document pages on heavy card stock. Cut the first sentence into strips (one strip equals one line of text). Shuffle the word strips, making sure they are not in sequence, and place them into a legal-size envelope. Label the envelope: Sentence #1. Continue to print and cut the remaining sentences. Place each sentence in its own numbered envelope, and label each envelope.

Step 5

Place the Sentence Puzzler envelopes at the front of the classroom. Students working in groups of three to four will retrieve one envelope at a time. Working together, the group will remove the sentence fragments and attempt to assemble the individual pieces as complete sentences.

Step 6

After the sentence fragments have been sequenced and a sentence has been constructed, have students record (write) the sentence in their journals. As students finish each sentence, have them pick up the sentence pieces, shuffle them, and return them to the Sentence Puzzler envelope. Have students bring the envelopes to the front of the classroom.

Step 7

Ask students to take another envelope, one at a time, until all sentences have been assembled and recorded. Note: if the sentences are recorded in sequence, the students will have a coherent paragraph.

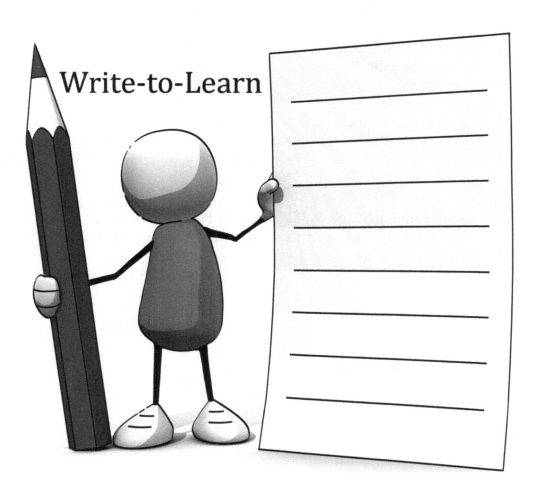

Write-to-Learn

Observe students as they attempt to build sentences. If they struggle, offer the following tips:

Tips for Solving Sentence Puzzlers

1. The first step is to look for a capital letter because it identifies the beginning of a sentence.
2. The second step is to look for a punctuation mark because it identifies the last part of a sentence.
3. The next step is to lay random pieces alongside the first fragment. Then groups can read the two joined fragments aloud and in sequence. After reading the fragments together, the group may decide that they don't sound right or reasonable. Then changes can be made. If it does sound right, the piece stays in its place, and the next piece is randomly placed and read. If that piece does not work, it is removed and another piece is tried in its place. The process continues until all fragments are used and the sentence is complete and correct.
4. Note that changes can be made in sentence arrangements at any point. Reading the sentences aloud is critically important because it allows students to hear, as well as see, the language. Frequently, students will comment, "That just doesn't sound right," or "That sounds right to me."

Some students, particularly ELLs, might benefit from a quick lesson before Sentence Puzzlers begins about sentence structure and syntax. Help students identify the five basic patterns around which most English sentences are built and provide these examples (see Table 6.1).

Table 6.1 Five Basic Structures of Simple Sentences

Subject-Verb	Mary talks.
Subject-Verb-Object	Dan is eating an apple.
Subject-Verb-Adjective	Henry is funny.
Subject-Verb-Adverb	Snow is everywhere.
Subject-Verb-Noun	Ms. Smith is the teacher.

Follow-up Activities

After the Sentence Puzzlers have been arranged and constructed, there are many creative ways to recycle this activity. Reusing Sentence Puzzlers in other ways can continue to boost confidence and improve the skills students need to read academic text. Here are some great follow-up ideas.

1. Use Sentence Puzzlers as a warm-up activity. Select a group of students to come forward. Let them select one envelope and have them assemble the sentence in front of the class, each student holding one fragment in each hand. After the group has assembled the pieces, the rest of the class choral reads the sentence aloud. The class gives a thumbs up if the sentence is correct or a thumbs down if they think it is incorrect. The class can offer suggestions and provide support if corrections need to be made.

2. Students are divided into four groups. Each group gets one Sentence Puzzler envelope and takes it to a designated corner of the classroom. Groups assemble the sentences by holding the pieces in their hands and placing themselves into the proper sentence sequence. When all groups are finished, the class choral reads each sentence aloud. Called *Read Around the Room*, this activity incorporates movement, collaboration, and reading. Students love it! Using the *popcorn reading* technique, students can lift each segment as it is read, and this keeps the readers visually on track. What's not to love about *popcorn reading* with your classmates?

DID YOU KNOW? . . .

Choral reading can build fluency. Choral reading involves students reading in unison with a fluent reader. This instructional strategy can be adapted for use with students at any grade level. As groups choral read, more fluent readers provide support for less fluent readers, allowing struggling readers to achieve success, even on difficult passages. During a choral read, less fluent readers can participate without fear of embarrassment as they practice reading aloud with the group. The teacher might begin by reading the text aloud to model fluency, as students visually follow the text. After the teacher models, students read the passage aloud together. Successive readings may occur over several sessions until students are able to read the passage independently (Rasinski, 2003).

3. Place the Sentence Puzzler envelope at learning centers for small groups to assemble, read, and record. Students can then:

   ◆ summarize the sentences in their own words;
   ◆ research the meaning of bold academic terms;
   ◆ write a new sentence using the bold academic terms;
   ◆ research the meaning of italicized processing words;
   ◆ write a new sentence using the italicized words in a different context;
   ◆ draw a graphic representation of the sentence;
   ◆ improve the paragraph by adding additional sentences.

Frequently Asked Questions

How often should I use Sentence Puzzlers in the classroom?

Sentences Puzzlers are a great way to introduce students to a new chapter. I also like to use this strategy after pre-teaching a set of key vocabulary terms. Sentence Puzzlers present newly introduced words in context and provide practice speaking, reading, and writing using the new vocabulary. Because the steps are performed quickly, it could be a weekly practice.

DID YOU KNOW? . . .

Seventy percent of all reading is done by only 10 percent of the population (Sanders, 1994). Using targeted strategies teachers can dramatically impact how much students read (Gambrell, 1996). Relatively simple strategies that increase student opportunities for reading, have a powerful effect on students' comprehension, thinking, knowledge of the world, and choices in higher education and life careers (Shefelbine 1998).

Are Sentence Puzzlers good for any grade level?

Yes. The complexity and language used in the Sentence Puzzler can be geared to any grade level. The strategy might sound elementary but secondary students willingly participate and enjoy the process. Sentences Puzzlers get sleepy teenagers up, moving, and reading "textbook" talk. In addition, with repeated use, key academic points are revisited, making them memorable.

What Research Has to Say

Reading fluency is a critical factor necessary for reading comprehension. Fluent readers are more likely to comprehend and remember the material because they read without difficulty (Rasinski, 2000). Students will build fluency when:

◆ teachers model good (fluent) oral reading;
◆ more fluent readers provide oral support as in a choral reading;
◆ students have many opportunities to practice reading aloud.

Research has shown that oral reading leads to better silent, independent reading. However, silent, independent reading does not necessarily lead to increased fluency and reading achievement (Armbruster, Lehr, & Osborn, 2001).

DID YOU KNOW? . . .

The more students read the better they read. "Reading volume—the amount students read in and out of school—significantly affects the development of reading rate and fluency, vocabulary, general knowledge of the world, overall verbal ability and last, but not least, academic achievement" (Cunningham & Stanovich, 1998). Readers must read extensively in text they can and want to read to gain fluency.

Tips to Consider for ELLs

✓ Place ELLs with students who are willing to offer support.
✓ Beginning speakers can be permitted to observe and listen as groups read and assemble sentences.
✓ Instruct beginning ELLs in how to select the first and last sentence fragments by looking for capital letters and punctuation marks.
✓ Encourage participation in choral reading of the sentences.

Activities that build fluency are particularly important for ELLs. ELLs must develop sight vocabulary and word knowledge while simultaneously gaining proficiency in oral language. They need support and many, many opportunities for practice!

Walk, Talk, Write, and Post

Teacher Journal

Walking and Talking to Learn

Current neuroscience research confirms that movement and cognition are powerfully connected. It also confirms that the age-old sit and get method, so frequently used for instruction, is difficult for the brain. If, as research documents, movement combined with instruction strengthens learning, elevates learner motivation and participation, and improves long-term memory and retrieval, why aren't students moving more while learning in the classroom? One simple answer is that teachers need more effective strategies for combining movement and instruction. They thirst for strategies that provide structured opportunities for students to move and learn and that don't disrupt and distract from the learning process.

After decades of teaching middle school students, I am aware of the fear teachers experience when students get out of their seats and start moving around the classroom. It doesn't take much for chaos to ensue if activities are not carefully structured and practiced. As noted in Numbered Heads, it is difficult to engage students in meaningful discussions about content. It is even more challenging to get students to use academic language while speaking and writing about content. The thought of adding movement to the process can be frightening, particularly for a novice teacher. One simple solution is a strategy I call, Walk, Talk, Write, and Post. It gets students moving, talking, sharing, reflecting, and writing. After hours of being parked in uncomfortable classroom chairs, this strategy gets both blood and ideas circulating!

Here's how it works . . .

Walk, Talk, Write, and Post combines movements and cognition that generate academic conversations and produce formal written responses. The strategy is simple and can be employed at any grade level in any content area. The process is student-centered, engaging, and it provides meaningful

opportunities for students to listen, speak, read, and write about content using academic language. In addition, the structure ensures that chaos doesn't erupt each time you use it!

The steps are as follows:

Step 1

Pose a thought-provoking question related to content. I like to start my questions with, "I was wondering . . ." It is important to ask the open-ended question in a manner that suggests you are genuinely interested in hearing what students are thinking. A math teacher starting a unit on geometric shapes might ask, "I was wondering what would happen if all the rectangles in this classroom suddenly disappeared?" A biology teacher might ask, "I was wondering, if you had to vote in favor of or against a law banning stem cell research, how would you vote and why?" An English teacher might ask, "I was wondering, if you selected a classmate to play the role of (name of main character in novel), who would you pick and why?" Questions can be structured to:

1. introduce a new content strand;
2. facilitate student thinking and speaking about newly introduced content;
3. encourage students to explore how learned concepts could be applied to solve new problems.

Step 2
Post a written sentence starter/stem to kick off the conversation.

If all the rectangles in this classroom suddenly disappeared . . .
If I were to vote on stem cell research, I would vote . . . because . . .
If I selected a classmate to play the role of . . . , I would pick . . . because . . .

Step 3
Provide background information or further explanation before student discussions, as needed. For example, a student might ask:

1. What does a rectangle look like? Is it the same as a square?
2. Where do stem cells come from? I don't remember what you said about them?
3. Is the . . . (main character) you are talking about the one who . . . ?

Teachers can verbally provide background information, even if not requested. In some instances, students can be given a short passage or illustration to read prior to discussions. The passage should provide background knowledge that will lead to a more productive conversation. When students know that they will be sharing their thoughts with others, they are more likely to seek out information and knowledge before beginning their conversations.

Step 4

Walk and talk about the question starting with the sentence starter/stem. Have students stand and walk towards the classroom door. As they reach the door, the person closest to them becomes their shoulder partner. The pairs of students proceed out the door forming a line. This could jokingly be referred as "the wedding march." The students follow a predetermined path, while they discuss the question and take turns sharing their thoughts. It is recommended that teachers have three designated paths:

- Short, for simpler questions: This can be a walk around the perimeter of the classroom. The number of times can be determined ahead of time.
- Medium, for intermediate questions: This walk can be inside the building but outside the classroom.
- Long, for complex questions: This can be an outside route . . . around the school track or other scenic loop.

After the route is completed, students return directly to their seats. At this point, all talking stops, and writing begins.

Step 5

Starting with the sentence starter/stem, students respond to the question in writing. Questions that can be answered with two to four sentences can be written on a sticky note and posted on the wall or whiteboard. Longer, written responses can be recorded on a half or quarter sheet of paper and posted immediately upon completion. Students can squeeze a lot of "thinking" onto a small piece of paper, and it is very important that the responses be posted. They can be taped to the whiteboard, pinned to a bulletin board, or laid out in a designated spot for the teacher and others to view. Written responses that are turned in and not posted result in interior responses. When a response is posted, the expectation is that several people will read it and respond to it. In other words, it is not going to quietly disappear into a stack of papers to be graded at some later time. Trust me, students understand the impact and the purpose of posting their ideas and thoughts. Check their Facebook pages, and you will see what I mean!

Frequently Asked Questions

Are there variations of the Walk, Talk, Write, and Post strategy I can use in the classroom?

Yes, there are many variations of Walk, Talk, Write, and Post. All provide increased opportunities for students to practice using newly acquired academic vocabulary in relevant contexts. Here are a few variations for teachers to consider:

1. **Walk, Talk, Draw, Post**: This variation uses the same format as Walk, Talk, Write, and Post but students are asked to *draw an*

illustration to show understanding instead of writing. For example, if the posted question is, "How can plants produce their own food?" students would walk and talk about the question and then draw a picture representing their understanding of photosynthesis. Students should be encouraged to add labels and notes to their drawings to clarify their thinking.

2. **Walk, Talk, Perform**: Again, this variation uses the same format as Walk, Talk, Write, and Post but students *perform a skit* to show understanding instead of writing. Skits are fun for the performer and often enlightening and entertaining for the audience. In addition, these short performances allow students to express their thinking and reveal what they know or do not know about a specific topic or word. For example, a teacher might ask students to walk, talk, and prepare a short skit about the words *simile* and *metaphor*. After returning to the classroom, students are given a few minutes to rehearse. As skits are performed classmates attempt to explain how the skit and the words might be connected. The class gradually comes to the conclusion that a simile is a metaphor, but not all metaphors are similes! At the conclusion, two important literary terms have been compared and contrasted and many *student examples* have been offered.

   Read, Talk (maybe Walk), Reread, Post: First, students read a passage independently or with a partner. They make annotated notes in the margin as they read.

Annotations can include:

√   Something I already know
NL   Something new I learned
Q   Question I have
?   I'm confused and don't get this
*   This is important information
!   This surprised me
R   This reminds me of . . .

Second, students work in pairs as they think and talk about the passage using question prompts such as:

◆   What is this passage about?
◆   What might the reader learn from reading this passage?

- ◆ Did you see any unfamiliar words? If yes, what do you think they might mean?
- ◆ Did reading this passage remind you of anything you already know about?
- ◆ Did any piece of information surprise you? If yes, what was it?
- ◆ If you had to summarize this passage in one to three sentences, what would you write?

Third, students reread the passage adding additional annotations. Finally, students respond to the question prompts in writing or are allowed time for a free write using a new prompt. Remember, if students are required to post and share their writing, compliance increases and quality improves. Also, if you need to get students up and moving, have students walk while they talk!

DID YOU KNOW? . . .

A brisk walk increases heart rate, promotes electrical activity in the brain, and releases excitatory brain chemicals. In other words, walking wakes up the brain, making its owner more alert. Essentially, it primes the pump for thinking and learning! For that matter, just standing and stretching increases blood flow from 5 to 8 percent. Recent studies reveal that exercise enhances memory, transfer of information, neuron connections, and plasticity . . . all critically important factors associated with learning (Tong, Shen, Perreau, Balazs, & Cotman, 2001).

Tips to Consider for ELLs

Teachers should:

- ✓ pair ELLs with other students in order to support and encourage speaking;
- ✓ allow ELLs to pair with other ELLs for this activity;
- ✓ provide, when possible, translated text of the question for beginning speakers;

✓ allow beginning speakers to discuss and respond to the question in their native language;

✓ remember the goal: to grow content knowledge as language skills are developing.

What Research Has to Say

One study found that making eye contact increases resistance to persuasion (Chen, Minson, Schöne, & Heinrichs, 2013). While students seated face-to-face may be more confrontational and more fixed in their viewpoints, students who walk together, side by side, almost always walk in rhythm. When they are in sync, they tend to be more collaborative, better listeners, and more open-minded.

A second study (Oppezzo & Schwartz, 2014) documents that walking indoors or outdoors boosts creative inspiration. Creativity levels are consistently and significantly higher for individuals who are walking, as compared to those who are sitting. That's right. Researchers suggest that you "Give your ideas some legs!"

In summary, the best way to become a better reader is to read more. And the best way to understand what we read is simply to talk, think, and write about it. We must increase student-to-student opportunities for reading, talking, and writing about content in the classroom. And don't forget, artistic responses to readings, such as drawings, skits, and songs have added value too!

7

21 Games and Extension Activities to Use with Card Sorts

After students complete a Card Sort activity, carefully following the six steps outlined, it is time to consider some games and extension activities using the cards. Remember, repeated exposure to the new words, pictures, and definitions is essential for student retention. New words become REAL words when they are spoken, described, read, and used in writing. The following games and activities ensure that students have expanded opportunities to use and develop the academic language they need to achieve success in school.

#1 Quick Draw

Why Play?
Quick Draw promotes quick thinking, and it encourages students to take academic risks. It also strengthens word knowledge, definitions, and image connections.

Directions
Step 1: Divide students into groups of three.

Step 2: Have students remove the pictures and vocabulary words, leaving only the definition cards in the bag.

Step 3: Next, have students scatter the vocabulary words and pictures on their tables, right side up.

Step 4: Ask one student to serve as a host. The host removes one definition card from the bag and reads it aloud.

Step 5: Upon hearing the definition, the other two students race to pick up the word and picture that matches the definition.

Step 6: The host announces the correct word and picture. Students holding the correct cards keep them and earn one point per card. If students pick up an incorrect card, they lose a point and return the card to the table.

Step 7: When both the correct word and picture are chosen, the definition card is removed from the stack, and the host continues. If an incorrect match is made and the card is returned, the definition card goes back into the bag. It will be read again later.

Step 8: When all cards have been correctly matched and picked up, the student with the highest number of points becomes the host for the next round.

#2 Concentration

Why Play?
Playing Concentration develops critical attention, focus, and memory. It also strengthens connections between a word, a graphic representation of the word, and its definition.

Directions

Step 1: Place students in groups of three.

Step 2: Select eighteen cards from a single *Vocabulary Magic™* Card Sort to play the game of Concentration. The game can be played with picture and word cards, word and definition cards, or definition and picture cards . . . any combination will work.

Step 3: Shuffle the eighteen cards and place them face down on the table.

Step 4: The first student turns over two cards in an attempt to find a match. If a match is made, the student keeps the cards and gets a second turn. If no match is made, the cards are turned face down again and play continues.

Step 5: For an extra challenge, students can play the game with all 27 cards. In this version of the game, allow students to turn over three cards at a time, attempting to find the word, picture, and definition cards that match. This is a great game for reviewing key vocabulary terms and building working memory!

#3 Pencil Points

Why Play?

Data collected from Pencil Points can be used as a formative assessment for word knowledge. Additionally, students can use the data for self-assessment. As students finish the first round of Pencil Points, encourage them to correct mistakes and play a second round. Students can track their progress and record their successes!

Directions

Step 1: Give students a piece of paper and a pencil.

Step 2: Have students number their papers with the number of vocabulary words they will be studying today.

Step 3: Read and show the definition of a vocabulary word.

Step 4: Have students write the vocabulary word that matches the definition.

Step 5: Continue until all words have been identified.

Note: Students get 1 point for each correct response.

#4 Picture This

Why Play?

Picture This is a student favorite. The competitive environment it creates boosts enthusiasm and increases student participation. Its format encourages students to brainstorm and think creatively about new words.

Step 1: Divide the class into two groups—girls vs. boys is fun.

Step 2: Select two students (one girl and one boy) from each group to come to the board.

Step 3: Select a vocabulary word from the bag and show it to the students at the board. The students at the board must draw a picture or graphic representation of the word—no words can be used, only pictures.

Step 4: After students draw their pictures, their teammates attempt to guess the word. The first group to correctly identify the word gets a point; the board is erased; and students return to their teams.

Step 5: The next two students come to the board, and the game continues until all words have been reviewed or time expires.

#5 Pass the Can

Why Play?
Music selected for Pass the Can elevates student mood and helps with word recall, especially when songs make the listener feel happy. The random selection of students for this activity heightens attentiveness to the task at hand.

Directions

Step 1: Choose some music for this game that students will enjoy.

Step 2: Place the vocabulary and definition cards in a container.

Step 3: Turn on the music.

Step 4: Have students pass the container to a neighbor until the music stops. The student holding the container must give it to the teacher.

Step 5: The teacher picks a card to show the student; the student identifies the definition if a word is shown; the student identifies the word if a definition is shown.

Step 6: Return the cards to the container and play continues.

Note: Students get one point for each correct response.

#6 Match, Match, Make a Match

Why Play?
Match, Match, Make a Match fosters cooperation among students. Movement during the activity enhances learning and allows for a quick check of student word knowledge (formative assessment). Repeated practice of the game provides time for students to relearn and self-correct.

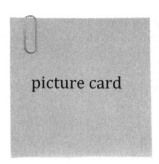  

Directions
Step 1: Each student is handed a picture, word, or definition card when entering the classroom.

Step 2: After all students are seated, the teacher gives the signal by saying, "Match, Match, Make a Match."

Step 3: Students get up and find the two other students in the classroom who have cards that match their card—it could be a picture, word, or definition card.

Step 4: The teacher quickly checks matches for accuracy. Each student then takes ten steps in any direction, stops, and exchanges cards with the nearest person.

Step 5: When the teacher says, "Match, Match, and Make a Match," students search again for the appropriate matches around the room. Play continues.

#7 Inside/Outside Circle of Words

Why Play?
Inside/Outside Circle of Words allows students to stand and move (in controlled movement activities) while they get instant feedback. Repeated practices of this kind will enhance word recall.

Directions

Step 1: Have students form two concentric circles—an inside circle and an outside circle—facing one another.

Step 2: The students in the inside circle hold a vocabulary word card and its companion definition card.

Step 3: The inside circle student reads the definition to the outside circle student, and he/she attempts to identify the word. If the student correctly identifies the word, the partner says, "Good job." If a mistake is made, the correct word is revealed, and the partner says, "You'll get it next time."

Step 4: When instructed, the outside circle rotates one person to the right while the inside circle remains still. Now, every student will have a new partner, and the process continues.

Note: Make sure there is ample spacing between students so they cannot overhear their neighbors' conversations.

#8 Pick Three

Why Play?

Pick Three gives students a chance to check their word knowledge as they construct simple and complex sentences to demonstrate relationships between words. In this cognitively challenging activity, students practice using core academic vocabulary.

Directions

Step 1: Have students work in groups of three.

Step 2: Place the vocabulary cards on the table, right side up.

Step 3: Within groups, the first student selects three picture cards from the table. The student sitting to his/her right must identify and pick up the corresponding word and definition cards.

Step 4: After the correct matches have been identified, the third student must construct a single sentence using the three words. This student then selects three more picture cards from the table and play continues, rotating to the left.

Note: To use this activity as a formative assessment, have students write their sentences on index cards.

 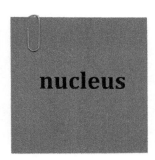 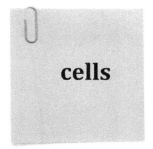

DNA in the **nucleus** of living **cells** contains the gentic code of life.

#9 I've Got Your Back

Why Play?

I've Got Your Back means that students will have an opportunity to tap prior knowledge to provide word hints to others. Students can listen, collect information, and search their memory banks to make an informed word decision as they circulate through the classroom. This activity involves movement and collaboration.

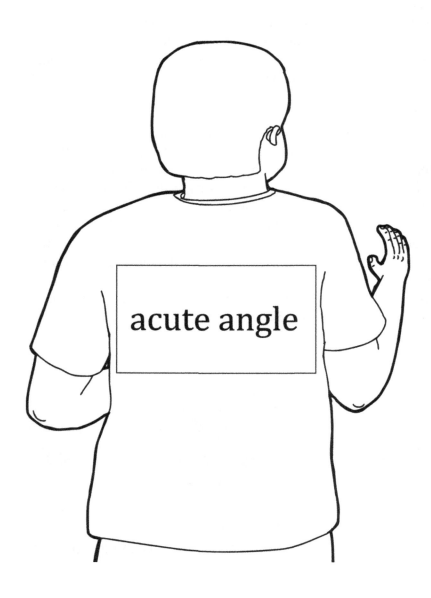

Directions

Step 1: The teacher clips a vocabulary card on the back of each student. The teacher keeps a few cards.

Step 2: Have students circulate through the room, asking other students to give them a hint about the word on their back. The student cannot ask questions, they can only listen to the hints.

Step 3: Have students tell the teacher when he/she knows the word.

Step 4: If the guess is correct, the teacher takes the word and replaces it with a new word.

Step 5: The teacher recirculates the words so that students are given multiple chances for review.

#10 Write It . . . Remember It

anything that has mass and takes up space

Why Play?

Write It . . . Remember It is a quick formative assessment that gives immediate feedback that directs future instruction. It offers opportunities to use correct spelling of academic vocabulary terms, reinforces recall, and deepens understanding of words. The competition in this activity sparks enthusiasm as students work individually or in pairs.

Directions

Step 1: Give students an individual whiteboard and dry erase marker.

Step 2: Read a definition card to students.

Step 3: Ask students to write the vocabulary word on their whiteboards that matches the definition read aloud.

Step 4: Ask students to hold up their whiteboards as soon as they have written the word.

Step 5: Give one point to the first student to write the word correctly.

#11 Word Map

Why Play?

A Word Map is a visual organizer that promotes vocabulary development. As students complete this word map, they develop a definition, synonym, antonym, and a complete sentence for new vocabulary terms.

Directions

Step 1: Students can work individually or with a partner for this activity.

Step 2: Give students a Word Map like the one above.

Step 3: Choose five vocabulary words for this activity.

Step 4: Have students complete the boxes, i.e., Word, Definition, Example (a synonym can be used here), and Sentence.

Note: To use this activity as a formative assessment, collect the Word Maps from students.

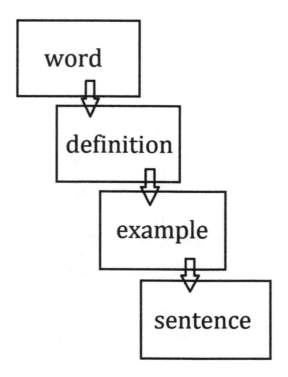

#12 Mind Reader

Why Play?
During Mind Reader, students construct good questions to help them discover the meaning of a word. As responses are given, students assess their knowledge and make an informed guess about the word in question.

Directions
Step 1: The teacher tells students there is a vocabulary word in his/her mind.

Step 2: Tell students they can ask yes/no questions about the word to help them identify the word. Students can choose to guess the word before the last student in class asks a question.

Step 3: When a student guesses the word, he/she cannot ask any more questions.

Step 4: When the word is correctly identified, the person next in line asks the first question about the next vocabulary word.

#13 Hot Seat

Why Play?

Being in the Hot Seat generates high levels of excitement and team building. Using gestures and kinesthetic movement . . . no oral language . . . students give word clues to the person in the hot seat so they can guess the vocabulary word.

Directions

Step 1: Divide the class into two teams and place a chair—a hot seat—at the front of the room.

Step 2: Have Team 1 choose a player to send to the hot seat.

Step 3: The teacher writes/displays a vocabulary word on the board behind the student sitting in the hot seat.

Step 4: Team 1 cannot talk but they can give clues about the word by using body gestures, kinesthetic movements, or by being creative without using oral language.

Step 5: When the student in the hot seat guesses the word correctly, Team 2 can send a student to the hot seat and the game begins again.

Note: Time in the hot seat can be limited.

#14 I Have . . . Who Has

Why Play?

Just before a vocabulary assessment, use I Have . . . Who Has. It's quick and easy . . . and perfect preparation!

Directions

Step 1: Use two sets of vocabulary cards for this activity. One set displays the word; the other set displays the definition.

Step 2: Distribute the vocabulary word cards to half the students in class; distribute the definition cards to the other half.

Step 3: Ask all students to stand up.

Step 4: Have the students with the word cards go first.

Step 5: Ask the first student to say, "I have . . . Who has what . . . means?"

#15 Everyday Tic-Tac-Toe

Why Play?
Using the classic Tic-Tac-Toe game plan, students can engage in a word review called Everyday Tic-Tac-Toe.

Directions
Step 1: Draw a large Tic-Tac-Toe grid on the board, and write a vocabulary word in each box.

Step 2: Divide the class into two teams of Xs and Os.

Step 3: Choose a starting team, and have the first person on that team explain the definition of a word on the Tic-Tac-Toe grid.

Step 4: If the definition is identified correctly, that team gets an X or O on the grid. The next team then gets a chance to play.

Step 5: The team with three Xs or Os in a row (horizontally, vertically, or diagonally) wins.

#16 Tic-Tac-Toe, Three Words in a Row

Why Play?

Tic-Tac-Toe, Three Words in a Row requires students to work together to compose complex sentences using academic vocabulary terms. This activity is cognitively challenging, requiring students to analyze relationships between words.

gene	**chromosome**	**DNA**
cell	**nucleus**	**code**
trait	**offspring**	**mutation**

Directions

Step 1: Remove nine word cards from the Card Sort bag.

Step 2: Place the words face up in a 3 x 3 design on the table.

Step 3: Have the first student select three words that are connected. The three words can be horizontal, vertical, or diagonal to each other.

Step 4: Students—working independently or as a team—must write a sentence using the three words; the sentence must explain the relationship among the words. For example, if the words selected are gene, DNA, and chromosome, the sentence might be: *Genes, located on chromosomes, are segments of DNA molecules that are the code for specific genetic traits.*

#17 Where Would You Find . . . ?

Why Play?

Where Would You Find . . . ? asks high-quality questions in a graphic organizer format. The questions promote brainstorming and collaboration, and they can be scaffolded so they increase in difficulty. In this activity, students generate original definitions, descriptions, or comparisons as they research available resources.

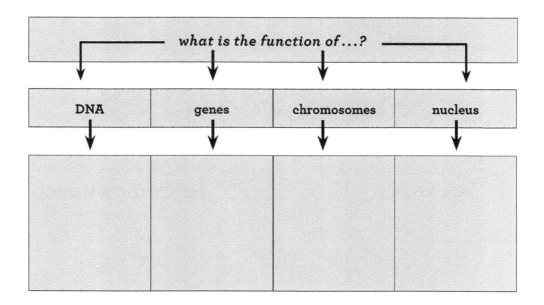

Directions

Step 1: Demonstrate how to use the Question Diagram graphic organizer above.

Step 2: Place students in groups of three.

Step 3: Write a question in the top box.

Step 4: Select four vocabulary words to insert in the second row.

Step 5: Have students write their responses after collaborating in their groups.

Step 6: Allow time for groups to share and/or for class discussion.

#18 Venn Diagram

Why Play?

Venn Diagrams are excellent opportunities for students to compare and contrast terms. During this activity, students are asked to review word meanings and to explore word relationships, as they describe how words are similar.

Directions

Step 1: Draw a Venn Diagram on the board and insert a vocabulary word on each side.

Step 2: Place students in groups of three to brainstorm descriptive words and phrases about each word. Similar characteristics of the words should be written in the middle section.

Step 3: Have students share their diagrams with the class.

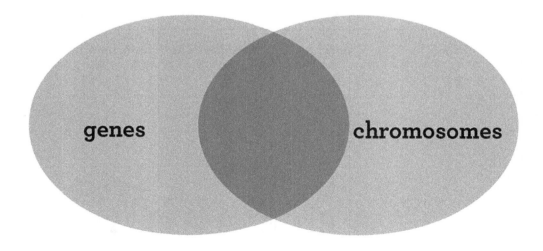

#19 Let's Get the Ball Rolling

Why Play?

Let's Get the Ball Rolling generates high levels of participation. During this activity, students practice listening skills as they exercise long-term-memory and recall. Teachers can easily assess student word knowledge as students participate.

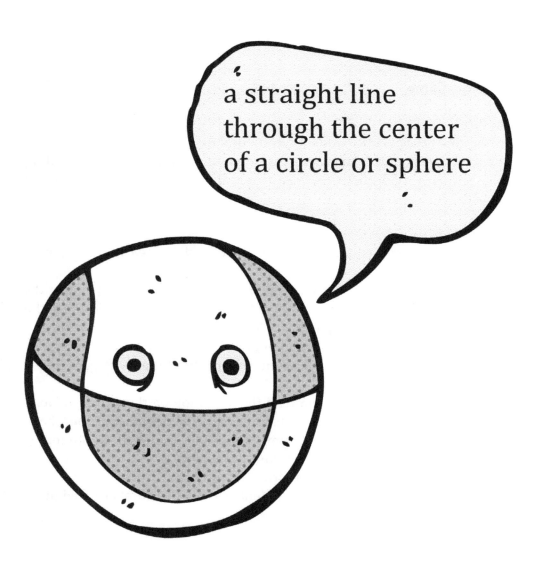

Directions

Step 1: Have students sit in a circle on the floor, facing inward. For older students, have them stand in a circle.

Step 2: The teacher holds a rubber ball in one hand, a vocabulary card in the other hand.

Step 3: The teacher rolls the ball to one student sitting in the circle, or the teacher throws the ball to one student standing in the circle.

Step 4: The student who receives the ball gives the definition for the vocabulary word.

Step 5: After a correct response, students listen for the next word. Then, he/she rolls/throws the ball to another student in the circle. Play continues.

#20 Dicey Game

Why Play?

During this Dicey Game, students read vocabulary definitions aloud while others say the word that matches. As students engage, they practice reading skills, reinforce connections between words and word meanings, and apply math skills to keep score!

Directions

Step 1: Place students in groups of three, and give each group paper, pencil, and dice.

Step 2: Give students a stack of definition and vocabulary word cards. Have students match the cards, clipping the definition to the back side of the corresponding term with a paperclip. The cards will now be "two-sided." Next place the cards on the table, definition side up.

Step 3: Have students in each group roll the dice to see who goes first—the highest number goes first.

Step 4: Have the first student read the definition on the top card. Next, ask the student to recall the word that matches that definition. If he/she is correct, a roll of the dice tells the number of points earned. If the student is unable to recall the vocabulary, no points are earned.

Step 5: The next player takes a turn.

Step 6: Play continues until a student reaches the number of winning points—usually 20–25.

#21 Index Bubbles

Why Play?

As students play Index Bubbles, they search for their vocabulary words in the index of their textbooks. Using the information they find, they can practice summarizing informational text.

Directions

Step 1: Have students look for Card Sort words in the indexes of books.

Step 2: Have students record the first three pages that list a reference to the vocabulary word as they find the word.

Step 3: Ask students to turn to each page referenced and search for the word in context.

Step 4: Have students record the new information in a bubble map like the one shown overleaf.

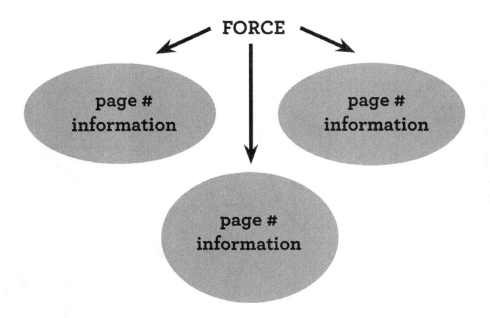

Remember...

Each new word of the Card Sort activity serves as an anchor for additional new words. With that understanding, the goal is to expand student understanding of the Card Sort words, without having students engage in rote memorization of vocabulary word definitions. Instead, students should participate in reading and writing activities using the new vocabulary words. Consider this last extension activity; I call it Index Bubbles. Students can complete this activity with little teacher support, and the benefits and skills practices are many. While doing Index Bubbles, students have the opportunity to:

✓ examine the parts of a textbook, including the index and glossary;
✓ locate and identify additional information as they scan academic text;
✓ practice summarizing textbook information in their own words;
✓ see new vocabulary words in context.

Anchor

Closing Thoughts

The strategies presented in *Making Words REAL* can be the cornerstone for building a language-rich, student-centered interactive classroom. When students work collaboratively and use academic language in listening, speaking, reading, and writing activities, those words become REAL and relevant. More importantly, the words they learn become part of meaningful conversations and learning accelerates.

The task of mastering academic language is a difficult one. In fact, it reminds me of a fable that I've taken the liberty to modify. It goes like this:

There was a rancher who had a dry water well on his property. Concerned about the liability of the open hole, he instructed his ranch hand to fill it in.

"If you want to keep your job, find that well, and fill it in," he said firmly.

Anxious to keep his job, the ranch hand located the open hole, picked up a load of dirt with his front-end loader, and started towards the well. As he approached the well, he heard a strange sound resonating from down below. Curious about the sound, he jumped off the tractor, walked over to the well, and much to his surprise he looked down and discovered his best horse at the bottom of the dry well.

"Oh shoot," he exclaimed. "How in the world did you end up down there?" The thought of burying his best horse alive with dirt made him shudder. Instead, the ranch hand reached for his shovel and threw a single scoop of dirt down into the hole. When the dirt hit the horse's back, he shook it off, and stomped on it. Seeing the horse's reaction made the ranch hand smile.

"That is one smart horse," he thought. "If I can sustain him with food and water while I shovel dirt into the hole, one scoop at a time, he can continue to shake and pound the dirt, gradually building up the ground beneath his feet. Slowly, but surely, that horse will rise up and one day that valued horse will be . . . on grade level!

If we want students to develop academic language, we must be careful not to bury them in an avalanche of new words. Instead, we can use proven strategies, teaching new words in small chunks, one Card Sort, one Picture Page, or one Vocabulary Bag activity at a time. Using highly effective strategies, students can build a solid foundation and have mastery of the words they need to succeed!

Appendix A

Vocabulary Magic™ Card Sort Instructions for Students

1. Sitting in groups of three, one of you takes all of the cards out of the plastic bag and sorts them into three neat stacks.

2. Place the picture cards back into the plastic bag.
3. Push the stack of definition cards off to the side. You will work with these cards later.
4. Spread the vocabulary terms out in a neat row across your table like this:

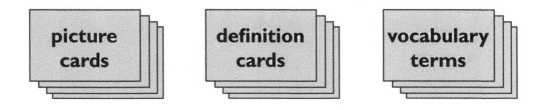

5. Your teacher will say (pronounce) each word aloud, and the class will repeat the word.

6. To start, the first student in your group removes one of the picture cards from the plastic bag, and he/she:

    a) describes the picture to your group using this stem: "In this picture, I see . . ." The student provides details about the word, but does not say the word;
    b) attempts to match the picture to one of the vocabulary terms by saying: "I think this picture might match the term . . . because . . .";
    c) places the picture under the vocabulary term;
    d) remembers to use the sentence stem and attempts to explain the match as clearly as possible.

7. After making a match, the bag passes to the next student, and the process of removing and matching the picture cards continues. Only one picture is removed at a time!

8. When all the picture cards have been matched to a term, drop the definition cards into the plastic bag and proceed with the same steps, until all matches are complete. Remember to use the sentence stems and to speak in complete sentences: "I think this definition might match the term . . . and this picture because . . ."

9. Watch the vocabulary trailer to check for accuracy. Make corrections by moving cards as needed.

10. When you are finished, select a Vocabulary Card Sort Game or Enrichment Activity to complete.

Appendix B

Vocabulary Magic™ **Word Journal**

Table A2.1

Word	Your Definition	New Information

Appendix C

Sentence Stems for Students

1. If I drew a picture to represent the word . . . it would look like . . .
2. . . . has the prefix/suffix/root . . . which means . . .
3. . . . is similar to . . . because . . .
4. . . . is different from . . . because . . .
5. When I hear the word . . . the picture that comes to mind is . . .
6. The word . . . reminds me of . . . because . . .
7. The word . . . means . . . not . . .
8. If I were explaining the word . . . to a friend, I would say . . .
9. The word . . . means . . . One example would be . . .

Appendix D

Vocabulary Card Template

References

Anderson, R. C., & Nagy, W. E. (1992). The vocabulary conundrum. *American Educator,* Winter, (14–18): 44–47.

Apthorp, H. (2006). Effects of a supplemental vocabulary program in third grade reading/language arts. *Journal of Educational Research,* 100(2): 67–79.

Armbruster, B., Lehr, F., & Osborn, J. (2001). *Put Reading First: The Research Building Blocks for Teaching Children to Read.* Washington, DC: National Institute for Literacy.

Asher, J. J. (2009). *Learning Another Language.* Los Gatos, CA: Sky Oak Productions.

Baddeley, A. D., & Longman, D. J. A. (1978). The influence of length and frequency of training sessions on the rate of learning to type. *Ergonomics,* 21(8): 627–635.

Bahrick, H. P., Bahrick, L. E., Bahrick, A. S., & Bahrick, P. E. (1993). Maintenance of foreign language vocabulary and the spacing effect. *Psychological Science,* 4(5): 316–321.

Baker, S., Simmons, D., & Kame'enui, E. (1998). *Vocabulary Acquisition: Synthesis of the Research.* Washington, DC: U.S. Department of Education, Office of Educational Research and Improvement, Educational Resources Information Center.

Beck, I. L., Perfetti, C. A., & McKeown, M. G. (1982). Effects of long-term vocabulary instruction on lexical access and reading comprehension. *Journal of Educational Psychology,* 74: 506–521.

Beck, I. L., McKeown, M. G., & Kucan, L. (2002). *Bringing Words to Life: Robust Vocabulary Instruction.* New York: Guilford Press.

Becker, W. C. (1977). Teaching reading and language to the disadvantaged—what we have learned from field research. *Harvard Educational Review,* 47: 518–543.

Bellon, J. J., Bellon, E. C., & Blank, M. A. (1992). *Teaching from a Research Knowledge Base: A Development and Renewal Process.* New York: Macmillan Publishing Company.

Biemiller, A. (2003). Vocabulary needed if more children are to read well. *Reading Psychology,* 24: 323–335.

Brady, T. F., Konkle, T., Alvarez, G. A., & Oliva, A. (2008). Visual long-term memory has a massive storage capacity for object details. *Proceedings of the National Academy of Sciences, USA*, 105(38): 14325–14329.

Chall, J. S., Jacobs, V. A., & Baldwin, L. E. (1990). *The Reading Crisis: Why Poor Children Fall Behind*. Cambridge, MA: Harvard University Press.

Chen, F. S., Minson, J. A., Schöne, M., & Heinrichs, M. (2013). In the eye of the beholder: Eye contact increases resistance to persuasion. *Psychological Science*, 24(11): 2254–2261.

Cook, S. W., Mitchell, Z., & Goldin-Meadow, S. (2008). Gesturing makes learning last. *Cognition*, 106(2): 1047–1058.

Cooper, J. D. (1997). *Literacy: Helping Children Construct Meaning* (3rd edn.). Boston: Houghton Mifflin.

Cunningham, A., & Stanovich, K. (1998). What reading does for the mind. *The American Educator*, Spring/Summer: 8–15.

Fisher, P., & Blachnowicz, C. (2005). Vocabulary instruction in a remedial setting. *Reading and Writing Quarterly*, 21: 281–300.

Gambrell, L. B. (1996). Creating classroom cultures that foster reading motivation. *The Reading Teacher*, 50: 235–262.

Goldin-Meadow, S. (2000). Beyond words: The importance of gesture to researchers and learners. *Child Development*, 71(1): 231–239.

Hart, B., & Risley, T. R. (2003). The early catastrophe: The 30 million word gap by age 3. *American Educator*, 27(1): 4–9.

Medina, J. (2008). *Brain Rules*. Seattle, WA: Pear Press.

Miller, G. A. (1956). The magical number seven, plus or minus two: Some limits on our capacity for processing information. *Psychological Review*, 63(2): 81.

Moats, L. (2001). Overcoming the language gap. *American Educator*, Summer: 5–9.

Oppezzo, M., & Schwartz, D. L. (2014). Give your ideas some legs: The positive effect of walking on creative thinking. *Journal of Experimental Psychology, Learning, Memory, and Cognition*, 40(4): 1142–1152.

Paivio, A., & Csapo, K. (1973). Picture superiority in free recall: Imagery or dual coding. *Cognitive Psychology*, 5(2), September: 176–206.

Perry, A. B. (2004). Decreasing math anxiety in college students. *College Student Journal*, 38(2): 321–324.

Rasinski, T. V. (2003). *The Fluent Reader: Oral Reading Strategies for Building Word Recognition, Fluency, and Comprehension*. New York: Scholastic.

Reeve, J., & Hyungshim, J. (2006). What teachers say and do to support students' autonomy during a learning activity. *Journal of Educational Psychology*, 98(1): 209.

Sanders, B. (1994). *A Is for Ox: Violence, Electronic Media, and the Silencing of the Written Word.* New York: Pantheon Books.

Shefelbine, J. (1998). *Academic Language and Literacy Development.* Paper presented at the 1998 Spring Forum on English Language Learners, Sacramento, CA.

Stafford, R., & Dunn, K.J. (1993). *Teaching Secondary Students Through Their Individual Learning Styles.* Columbus, OH: Allyn and Bacon.

Stahl, S., & Fairbanks, M.M. (1986). The effects of vocabulary instruction: a model based meta-analysis. *Review of Educational Research*, 56: 72–110.

Tong, L., Shen, H., Perreau, V.M., Balazs, R., & Cotman, C.W. (2001). Effects of exercise on gene-expression profile in the rat hippocampus. *Neurobiology of Disease*, 6: 1046–1056.

U.S. Department of Education, Institute of Education Sciences, National Center for Education Statistics, National Assessment of Educational Progress (NAEP), various years, 1971–2012, Long-Term Trend Reading Assessments.

White, T.G., Graves, M.F., & Slater, W.H. (1990). Growth of reading vocabulary in diverse elementary schools: Decoding and word meaning. *Journal of Educational Psychology*, 82(2): 281–290.